SPOKEN LEBANESE

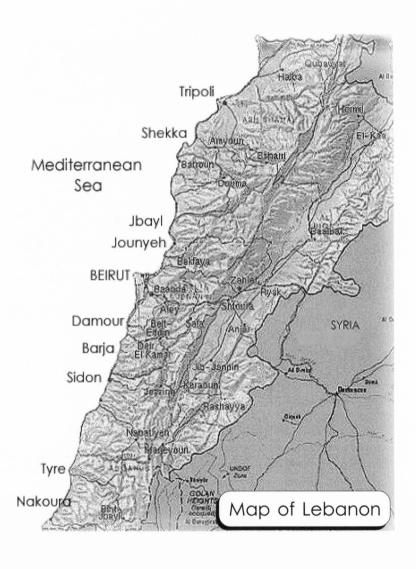

Map of Lebanon

SPOKEN
LEBANESE

Maksoud N. Feghali, Ph. D.

Parkway Publishers, Inc.
Box 3678, Boone, NC 28607

Published in the United States.

Library of Congress Cataloging-in-Publication Data

Feghali, Maksoud Nayef.
    Spoken Lebanese / Maksoud N. Feghali. —1st ed.
      p. cm.
    ISBN 1-887905-14-6
    1. Arabic language--Dialects--Lebanon. 2. Arabic
language--Conversation and phrase books--English.
I. Title.
PJ6810.3.F44 1999
492.7'7--dc21   99-10479
                                   CIP

First Edition

Book Design by Christopher Frisco
Cover Design by Christopher Frisco & Beth Jacquot

The pictures used to introduce chapters 3, & 6 through
15 were used with permission of the Lebanon Ministry
of Tourism.

ACKNOWLEDGEMENTS

To my mother Camilia, and the blessed soul
of my father Nayef for their inspiration;

To my wife Maguy, and my children Andrew,
Mario and Peter for being proud of our
heritage, and for their love, advice, and sacrifice;

To my dear colleague Dr. William Hutchins
for his sensitive and experienced
reading of this manuscript;

To my brother Elie, for his trust and
continuous encouragement;

To all my immediate family, brothers, sisters,
nephews, nieces, sisters-in-law, and their
families, for their support and feedback;

I am more grateful than I could ever say.

CONTENTS

INTRODUCTION

During the past century, many Lebanese emigrants have left home and sailed overseas looking for prosperity and better life conditions.

In recent years, the emigration wave has reached the point that more Lebanese are living abroad than in Lebanon. They have integrated fully in their host countries and played key roles in their new societies. Lebanon, despite its small area and population, has become very well known in the world. There is hardly any city that does not have a Lebanese restaurant or a small Lebanese community. Many Lebanese have married outside their culture and adapted to a new life style, but others have difficulties integrating their spouses into their own culture because of the language barrier. Many of us have experienced the unpleasant handicap of being around people who do not speak our language. In my immediate family, my three foreign born sisters-in-law often felt alienated when the conversation has shifted spontaneously into Lebanese.

Therefore, I decided to put my many years of experience as a professor of foreign languages to the service of my immediate family and my extended Lebanese family by authoring a simple conversational book. My goal is to help all those interested in learning the Lebanese dialect reach a comfortable level of proficiency that will provide them with basic survival skills and encourage them to become active speakers rather than passive listeners.

To reach this goal I rely on the following instructional tools:

a. A simple phonetic system
b. Short dialogues
c. Culture and Vocabulary Section
d. Grammar notes
e. Reinforcements

The phonetic system I adopted is a simplified adaptation of the IPA (International Phonetic Alphabet). It is intended to present the Arabic sounds in a contrastive way with European sounds, limiting the memorization of phonetic symbols to just a few.

The short communicative exchanges are based on real life situations and contain useful, high frequency vocabulary.

The vocabulary and culture section presents the learner with valuable cultural information in addition to detailed explanatory notes for the communicative exchanges.

Since my goal is to teach the Lebanese Dialect which is easily understood in Syria, Jordan, Palestine and other parts of the Arab World, I will avoid elaborate grammar notes related to MSA (Modern Standard Arabic) and I will focus closely on verb conjugational patterns and pronominal suffixes.

My intentions are not to discourage anyone from learning our beautiful Arabic Language. I am simply offering a survival package to those interested only in speaking our dialect.

Reinforcements will help the learner to go beyond the material presented in the chapter and use words from the supplementary list provided.

Since Lebanon lived many years under foreign occupation, it should be no surprise to the learner to encounter many familiar words such as "Sandwich", "Balcon", "Chauffeur" etc... . Lebanon has never opposed the integration of foreign words into its dialect. Those interested in this topic may consult my work *Lexicon of Foreign Words in the Syrian-Lebanese Dialect,* available at the Defense Language Institute in Monterey, California, and at Appalachian State University, Boone, North Carolina. They may also order it through the publisher of this book.

In conclusion, I hope that the learner find this work rewarding. I strongly encourage anyone who is eager to learn our beautiful dialect to seek the help of native speakers, to be linguistically inquisitive and aggressive, and to practice. Best wishes !

PHONETIC SYSTEM

In Modern Standard Arabic the phonological system consists of 28 consonants and 6 vowels. More than half of them are similar to English and are easy to pronounce.

Choosing a phonetic system for the Lebanese dialect is a complicated task because many integrated foreign words kept their original forms. Therefore I chose a simple modified system adopted from the IPA to satisfy the needs of our dialect without compromising the pronunciation of foreign words. This system will be presented in a clear way, in order to better help the learner who has no phonetic background. It is very important that you familiarize yourself with this system and you master the sounds before moving on to the first chapter.

CONSONANTS

b   ب   (be) boy, rib.

p   (p) park, rope (the p is not an Arabic consonant).

d   د   (daal) door, bid.

D   ض   (DaaD) This consonant is closely associated with Arabic which is also called: the language of DaaD. It is an emphatic velarized correlative of "d". To pronounce this sound, place the tip of the tongue against the upper teeth, stiffen the tongue and tighten the muscles of your throat.

t   ت   (te) tan, kit. Always dental.

T   ط   (Tah) It is a voiceless alveolar stop, while the plain /t/ is a dental stop. The tongue should be slightly retracted and raised towards the soft palate.

j   ج   (jiim) girafe, Asia.

g   (g) go, bag (The g is not an Arabic consonant, but it is present in the Egyptian dialect.)

k   ك   (kaaf) kilo, cup, back

G   غ   (Gayn) similar to the Parisian "r", the back of the tongue should be slightly raised towards the roof of the mouth as if you are gargling. The front of the tongue should remain tight and low. The stream of air will cause the vibration of the vocal cords.

'   ء   (hamza) air, on. It is a glottal stop that may occur in the beginning, in the middle or at the end of a word. In English, it occurs in monosyllable words, or in words that begin with a vowel followed generally by two consonants as in "absence, orbit". In certain areas, people use it instead of /t/ in the middle of a word as in "mutton". It is produced by closing and quickly opening the vocal cords.

Q   ق   (Qaaf) This sound is heard in some Lebanese areas namely the Shouf Mountains and the Bekaa Valley. It has been replaced by a glottal stop (') or Hamza in all other areas. It surfaces however in certain words where the glottal stop is closely followed by the Qaaf, like in "anaaQa" (elegance); or "ayQuune" (icon). It is a guttural "kaaf" produced from the back of the mouth. The back of the tongue should touch the uvular area, while the front part remains closely tight to the bottom of the mouth. Similar to "cough, call".

l   ل   (laam) lemon, mile; it is a non-velarized sound.

r   ر   (re)   rose, bar.

z   ز   (zayn)   zone, wise.

Z   ظ   (Zah)   It is an emphatic "z".

s   س   (siin)   sun, mice.

S   ص   (Saad)   It is an emphatic "s" produced by applying the tip of the tongue against the lower teeth while the back of the tongue is pressing against the velum, forcing the air to go through the tongue and the alveolar ridge.

ʃ   ش   (Shiin)   shine, fish, portion. It is the equivalent of "sh" in English and "ch" in French.

f   ف   (fe)   foot, roof, rough.

m   م   (miim)   moon, room.

n   ن   (nuun)   nun, fan.

h   ه   (he)   hay, hotel, hobby.

H   ح   (He)   This sound is similar to the sound produced when you clear your throat. It is a voiceless pharyngeal sound formed by constricting the walls of the pharynx while breathing.

x   خ   (xe)   Similar to the /ch/ in certain German words like "Nacht". It is a voice-

less velar and fricative sound. It is produced by narrowing the passageway
between the back of the tongue and the
velum. The front of the tongue remains
low. During the passage of air, the vocal cords are not vibrated.

9   ع   (9ayn) This consonant, like the /D/, /
T/, /G/, /Q/, /S/, /H/, and the
/x/ has no English equivalent. It is a
voiced pharyngeal and fricative sound.
It is produced by tightening the muscles
of the throat and expulsing the breath
through the vibrating vocal cords.

w   و   (waaw) water, vow. It is also a diph-
thong when preceded by /a/ as in
/tawm/ "twins".

y   ي   (ye) yes, say, oyster. It is also a diph-
thong when preceded by /a/ as in
/bayt/ "house".

VOWELS

---

a   Short vowel as in: baboon, part.

aa   Prolonged vowel as in: bar, far.

i   Short vowel as in: media, seashore.

ii   Prolonged vowel as in: beast, fleet.

u   Short vowel as in: book, should.

uu   Prolonged vowel as in: booth, soon.

e   Short vowel as in: neck, cell, bed.

ee   Prolonged vowel as in: man, bear.
                   (do not confuse with /ee/ in English)

œ   Vowel heard in foreign words like
                      chauffeur /ʃofœr/.

o   Vowel heard in foreign words like
                   Police /poliis/ or /boliis/.

**Please note that proper names are not capitalized.
They are preceded by an asterisk:**

e.g. *samiir, *maHmuud

Intonations and accents may vary from one Lebanese region to another, therefore the pronunciation of certain words may differ from the way they are phonetically transcribed in this book , e.g. /bayt/ "house" may be said /beyt/; /ana/ "me, I" may be said /ane/ in some areas; /layʃ/ "why" may be said /ley/, and the pronoun suffix /i/ may be pronounced /e/ or a sound in between /i/ and /e/ etc... While this may cause some listening comprehension difficulties, it should not affect the speaking competency of the learner.

Consonants are divided into "lunar" and "solar" depending on their behavior with the letter /l/ of the definite article "al". The /l/ remains with words beginning with a lunar consonants, e.g. "albayt" meaning: the house; it disappears with words beginning with solar consonants, leading to the doubling of that consonant, e.g. "aʃʃams" meaning: the sun. This is the reason why you may see two similar consecutive consonants in the communicative exchanges presented in this book. The transition between a word followed by another word that begins with a solar consonant is made easy sometimes by inserting a transitional vowel such as /a/, /i/, /u/, or /e/, e.g. "bayt e ʃʃa9b" meaning: the people's house; "ra'iis e ddawle" meaning the president of the state. All dental and palatal consonants are solar, with the exception of /j/ and /y/ which are lunar. In the Lebanese dialect the list of solar consonants is shorter than the list of MSA because certain consonants like ذ /th/ as in "those" and ث /th/ as in "earth" are absent. The followings are the solar consonants in the Lebanese dialect:
/t/, /T/, /d/, /D/, /r/, /z/, /Z/, /s/, /S/, /ʃ/, /l/, /n/.

Chapter One
Greetings & Formalities

In this chapter you will learn formal and informal greetings, formalities and etiquette. You will also learn pronouns, pronominal suffixes and some useful interrogatives.

FORMAL GREETINGS

In the morning: SabaaH-lxayr   "Good morning"
In the evening: masa-lxayr   "Good evening"

OTHER FORMS OF GREETING

assalaamu 9alaykum   "Peace be upon you"
marHaba   "Hi, Hello"
In the evening: sa9iide   "pleasant evening"
In a working environment:
9aweefe or ya9tiik-l9aafye "wishing you health"

If you are addressing someone in particular you may use the vocative (ya) before his/her name, e.g. marHaba ya *samiir.

In the following exchanges you will become familiar with some Lebanese names, and you will learn how to great people and answer their greetings.

*sa9iid: SabaaH-lxayr ya *9aaTif
*9aaTif: ahlan, SabaaH-nnuur ya *sa9iid

*9afaaf: masa-lxayr ya *Hanaan
*Hanaan: masa-nnuur ya *9afaaf

*Hasan: assalamu 9alaykum ya *9adnaan
*9adnaan: wa9alaykumu-ssalaam ya *Hasan

*xaaled: marHaba ya *hiʃaam
*hiʃaam: marHabtayn ya *xaaled

*sihaam: 9aweefe ya *huda
*huda: alla y9afiiki ya *sihaam

*9umar: sa9iide ya *Haliim
*Haliim: yis9ud ha-lmasa ya *9umar

Greetings are usually followed by common courtesy questions, e.g. (kifak) How are you? (kiif-lHaal) How is it going? etc. . . . Middle Easterns always thank (*alla) God for their well being.

*samiir: marhaba ya *salwa
*salwa: ahlan *samiir, kiifak?
*samiir: lHamdilla, kiifik inti?
*salwa: nuʃkur *alla meeʃe-lHaal

(ahlan) is an expression used to welcome someone, or to answer someone's greeting. It means literally: you are among your family.

(kiif) is an interrogative meaning "how". Verb "to be" is implied in pronouns or pronominal suffixes like ik, ak, etc. . . . Therefore (kiifak) means: how are you, masculine, singular .

(inti) is a feminine singular pronoun.

GRAMMAR NOTES

In this book I will use the following abbreviations:

masc.   Masculine

fem.	Feminine
sing.	Singular
pl.	Plural
perf.	Perfect
imperf.	Imperfect
imp.	Imperative
pron.	Pronoun
prep.	Preposition
lit.	Literally
leb.	Lebanese

Please note that in the leb. dialect the fem. pl. pron. and pronominal suffixes are replaced by the masc. pl. pron. and pronominal suffixes. The dual pron. are replaced by the masc. pl. pronouns. **In all examples of the explanatory notes, I used the masc. sing. form.**

PRONOUNS

he, him	huwwe
she, her	hiyyi
they, them	hinni
you (masc. sing.)	inta
you (fem. sing.)	inti
you (masc. & fem. pl.)	intu
I, me	ana
we, us	niHna

PRONOMINAL SUFFIXES

When pronominal suffixes are added to a noun they indicate possession; e.g. baytak (your home, masc. sing.), ismak (your name, masc. sing.); when added to a verb they are considered direct or indirect objects of that verb. e.g. ʃeefak (he saw you).

u	masc. sing. (his)	baytu	ismu
a	fem. sing.(her)	bayta	isma
un	masc. & fem. pl.(your)	baytun	ismun
ak	masc. sing. (your)	baytak	ismak
ik	fem. sing. (your)	baytik	ismik
kun	masc. & fem. pl. (your)	baytkun	ismkun
i	(my)	bayti	ismi
na	(our)	baytna	ismna

SOME USEFUL INTERROGATIVES

what	ʃu
who	miin
how	kiif
where	wayn
when	aymta
how much	'iddayʃ
why	layʃ
what does it mean	ʃu ya9ni
what is your name	ʃu ismak (masc. sing)
what is this	ʃu hayda

OTHER USEFUL VOCABULARY

yes	na9am
no	la'
if possible	iza mumkin
perhaps	bijuuz
correct, true	SaHiiH
of course	Tab9an
wrong, incorrect	GalaT
thank you	ʃukran
a reply to ʃukran	9afwan (do not mention it, you are welcome)

my name is	ismi
I want	baddi
here	hawne
give me	9Tiini
a little	ʃway
a lot	ktiir

NATIONALITIES

American	amerkeeni
Australian	ustraali
British	ingliizi
Canadian	kanadi
French	frinseewi
German	ulmaani
Lebanese	libneeni
Polish	poloni
Russian	ruusi
Spanish	spanyoli

REINFORCEMENT

• Practice the exchanges with a Lebanese speaker.

• Apply the pronominal suffixes to nouns like:
Haal (condition, state); ism (name); 9umr (age).

• Apply the pronominal suffixes to prepositions
like: ma9 (with, to have); 9ind (at, with, to have).

Chapter Two
Socializing & Family Members

In this chapter you will learn basic expressions used when you meet someone or family members for the first time. You will also become acquainted with codes of conduct when socializing with a Lebanese family.

The verbs conjugated in this chapter are:
tfaDDal, Habb, 9arraf, ∫irib, ∫akar

DIALOGUE I

*marwaan:	SabaaH-lxayr ya xeelti.
xeelit *marwaan:	SabaaH-nnuur ya 9ayni, tfaDDal.
*marwaan:	∫ukran ya xeelti. bHibb 9arrfik 9ala madaamti. isma *sandra, whiyyi amerkeniyyi.
xeelit *marwaan:	ahlan *sandra, t∫errafna. kiif Haalik?
*sandra:	lHamdilla, ktiir mniiHa.
xeelit *marwaan:	n∫alla mabsuuTa b*libneen?
*sandra:	na9am, ktiir mabsuuTa.
xeelit *marwaan:	tfaDDalu ∫rabu finjeen 'ahwe.
*marwaan:	mersi, bil'afraaH n∫alla. yalla bxaaTrik ya xeelti
xeelit *marwaan:	ma9-ssaleeme ya 'albi, alla ma9kun.

CULTURE & VOCABULARY

It is customary in Lebanon that when you pass by someone's house to be invited in. The expression "tfaDDal" follows automatically the greeting. If you are visiting with someone, you have to adhere to the following cultural norms:

• Do not put your feet on the coffee table or in any position facing other people.

• Do not help yourself to anything at the coffee table unless you are invited to.

• Do not ask for sodas or drinks, your host will offer you what is available in the house.

• When you meet someone for the first time, please use the expression "tʃarrafna" which means "I am honored to meet you".

• If another guest or a family member walks in or out of the living room, please stand up to greet him or to say "good bye" to him. It is rather rude to remain seated unless you are asked to do so.

• When requesting something from your host, please use one of the following expressions: "please", "9mul ma9ruuf" do me a favor, "min faDlak" if you please.

• If you decide to stand up and leave, or you would like to be excused for a moment, please use the expression "bil'izn" with your permission.

xeelti: my maternal aunt. xeele, maternal aunt. **It looses the /e/ and takes a /t/ before the pronominal suffix to avoid the collision of the two vowels.**

9ayni: my eye. Some people, especially the older ones use terms of endearement when talking to their relatives or to the younger ones. You may hear "ya 'albi" my heart, "ya ruuHi" my soul, etc... .

tfaDDal: come in, lit. be generous. Imp. of tfaDDal. See grammar notes for conjugation.

bHibb: I would like, I love. Imperf. of Habb (to like, to love). See grammar notes.

9arrfik: introduce you. Imperf. of 9arraf (to introduce), with the pronominal suffix "ik". This verb is usually followed by the preposition "9ala" which means: to, on.

madaamti: From French "madame", my wife. The word "marti" is also used.

isma: her name. ism: name.

amerkeniyyi: American (fem.), amerkeeni (masc.), amerkeen (pl.).

tʃarrafna: nice to meet you. Perf. of tʃarraf (to be honored), conjugated like tfaDDal.

mniiHa: fine, good (fem.), mniiH (masc.), mneeH (pl.).

mabsuuTa: happy (fem.), mabsuuT (masc.), mabsuuTiin (pl.).

*libneen: Lebanon. The b that precedes it is a preposition meaning: in.

ktiir: very, too much, a lot.

ʃrabu: drink, imp. of ʃirib (to drink). See grammar notes.

finjeen: cup, fnejiin (pl.).

'ahwe: coffee.

mersi: from French (merci), thank you.

bil'afraaH: in happy occasions. (may we drink your
                  coffee in happy occasions).

yalla: interjection meaning, OK now, let's go,
                  come on. yalla yalla: means hurry up,
                  move it.

bxaaTrik: with your permission, good by now(fem.),
                  bxaaTrak (masc.), bxaaTurkun (pl.).

ma9:   prep. with.

saleeme: safety. ma9-ssaleeme: good bye, lit. go
                  with safety.

'albi: my heart.

The hyphen that connects the two words marks the absence of the definite article "al", and the doubling of the initial consonant as seen in the phonetic remarks. It indicates that the two words should be pronounced as one. This will prevent glottal stops and mispronunciations.

DIALOGUE II

*samia: masa-lxayr ya 9ammi.
*saliim: ahlan, masa-nnuur, kiif-SSuHHa?
*samia: 9aal, nuʃkur *alla. bHibb 9arrfak 9ala
              jawzi *lari, huwwe ingliizi.
*saliim: ahlan ya *lari, ilna-ʃʃaraf.
*lari: biHadrtak ya 9amm.
*saliim: kiif, nʃalla mabsuuT b*libneen?
*lari: ma9luum, ktiir mabsuuT.

*saliim:	bitHibbu tiʃrabu finjeen 'ahwe?
*samia:	Gayr marra nʃalla. yalla bxaaTrak.
*saliim:	ma9-ssaleeme, alla ma9kun.

Culture & Vocabulary

9amm:

paternal uncle. 9ammi (paternal aunt).
The /i/ after 9amm is a pronominal suffix.

SuHHa:

health. kiif-SSuHHa is another way of
saying "how are you?".

9aal:

fine, well.

nuʃkur:

we thank, imperf. of ʃakar (to thank). See
grammar notes.

jawzi:

my husband. Some people use the word
"xaweejti".

ingliizi:

British, English.

ilna:

lit. for us, belongs to us. This expression is
made of the prep."ila" for, and the pronominal suffix "na".

ʃaraf:

honor.

biHaDrtak:

lit. in your presence, nice to meet you too,
like wise. HaDrat is a respectful and an
official way to address someone or a
dignitary.

ma9luum:

of course, sure.

Gayr:

another.

marra: time, once, marraat (pl.).

GRAMMAR NOTES

In Arabic, the third masc. sing. form of the perfect tense is the root of the verb; e.g. "ʃirib" he drank, is the root of verb to drink; "daras" he studied, is the root of verb to study. In the Vocab. notes, the root will be given after the tense.

Verbs in Arabic are commonly divided into triliteral (three letters) and quadriliteral (four letters) verbs. There are very few exceptions to that rule.

The triliteral verbs are divided into ten **Measures** according to their pattern of conjugation. Quadriliteral verbs have only two common measures.

If the root of a triliteral verb has a /w/or a /y/ in the beginning, the verb is called: **Assimilated**, e.g. wa9ad: to promise.

If the root of a triliteral verb has a vowel in the middle, the verb is called: **Hollow**, e.g. neem: to sleep; raaH: to leave, to go.

If the root of the triliteral verb ends with a vowel, the verb is called **Defective**; e.g. bi'i: to stay, to last; nisi: to forget.

The most frequent verbs are **Measure I** verbs which have a simple and predictable pattern of conjugation in the Perfect and Imperfect tenses and in the Imperative.

The other most common measures are: Measure II which causes generally someone to do something; Measure III which adds a meaning of reciprocity to Measure I; Measure V which causes the verb to be reflexive; Measure VII which adds passivity to the verb; Measure IX associated mainly with colors; and Measure X which often adds reflexivity or inquisition to the meaning of the verb.

The following is the conjugation of verbs you have seen in this chapter:

• **tfaDDal (to come in, to be generous)** is a Measure V verb.

Pronoun	Perfect	Imperfect	Imperative
huwwe	tfaDDal	yitfaDDal	
hiyyi	tfaDDalit	titfaDDal	
hinni	tfaDDalu	yitfaDDalu	
inta	tfaDDalt	titfaDDal	tfaDDal
inti	tfaDDalti	titfaDDali	tfaDDali
intu	tfaDDaltu	titfaDDalu	tfaDDalu
ana	tfaDDalt	itfaDDal	
niHna	tfaDDalna	nitfaDDal	

If the imperfect tense is not preceded by another verb, it takes a /b/ in the beginning (except with niHna it takes /m/) . This indicates a habitual or a repetitive act, e.g. byitfaDDal, mnitfaDDal; bHibb, minHibb.

If the imperfect is preceded by the prefix "9am" it indicates an action in progress.

The Imperfect may sometimes refer to a future act depending on the context.

In order to form the future tense of any verb, you add "raH" to the imperfect.

• **Habb (to love, to like)** is a doubled verb, it ends with two similar consonants.

Pronoun	Perfect	Imperfect	Imperative
huwwe	Habb	yHibb	
hiyyi	Habbit	tHibb	
hinni	Habbu	yHibbu	

inta	Habbayt	tHibb	Hibb
inti	Habbayti	tHibbi	Hibbi
intu	Habbaytu	tHibbu	Hibbu

| ana | Habbayt | Hibb |
| niHna | Habbayna | nHibb |

• **9arraf (to introduce)** is a Measure II verb.

Pronoun	Perfect	Imperfect	Imperative
huwwe	9arraf	y9arrif	
hiyyi	9arrafit	t9arrif	
hinni	9arrafu	y9arrfu	
inta	9arraft	t9arrif	9arrif
inti	9arrafti	t9arrfi	9arrfi
intu	9arraftu	t9arrfu	9arrfu
ana	9arraft	9arrif	
niHna	9arrafna	n9arrif	

• **ʃirib (to drink)** is a sound Measure I verb.

Pronoun	Perfect	Imperfect	Imperative
huwwe	ʃirib	yiʃrab	
hiyyi	ʃirbit	tiʃrab	
hinni	ʃirbu	yiʃrabu	
inta	ʃribt	tiʃrab	ʃraab
inti	ʃribti	tiʃrabi	ʃrabi
intu	ʃribtu	tiʃrabu	ʃrabu
ana	ʃribt	iʃrab	
niHna	ʃribna	niʃrab	

• **ʃakar (to thank)** is a sound Measure I verb.

Pronoun	Perfect	Imperfect	Imperative
huwwe	ʃakar	yiʃkur	
hiyyi	ʃakarit	tiʃkur	
hinni	ʃakaru	yiʃkru	
inta	ʃakart	tiʃkur	ʃkur
inti	ʃakarti	tiʃkri	ʃkiri
intu	ʃakartu	tiʃkru	ʃkiru
ana	ʃakart	iʃkur	
niHna	ʃakarna	niʃkur	

OTHER USEFUL VOCABULARY

Demonstratives

this, masc. sing.	hayda, e.g. hayda *saliim (this is *saliim).
this, fem. sing.	haydi, e.g. haydi *samia (this is *samia).
these, masc. & fem. pl.	hawdi, e.g. hawdi *samia w*saliim (these are *samia and *saliim).
those, masc. & fem. pl.	hawdiik, e.g. hawdiik *samia w*saliim (those are *samia and *saliim).

Conjunction

and	/w/ e.g. *saliim w *samia (*saliim and *samia).

Family Members & Relatives

For an extended list please look at the appendix.

father	bayy, bayyeet (pl.)
mother	imm, immeet (pl.)
brother	xayy, ixwe (pl.)
sister	uxt, xayyeet (pl.)
son	ibn, wleed (pl.)
daughter	bint, baneet (pl.)
grand father	jid, jduud (pl.)
grand mother	sit, sitteet (pl.), (it also means lady, or Mrs.)
uncle	9amm (paternal side), 9muum (pl.) xeel, (maternal side), xweel (pl.).
aunt	9ammi (paternal side), 9ammeet (pl.); xeele (maternal side), xeleet (pl.).

REINFORCEMENT

- Answer the following questions:

1. kiif Haalak /Haalik?
2. inʃalla mabsuuT/mabsuuTa blibneen?
3. bitHibb/bitHibbi tiʃrabi finjeen 'ahwe?
4. bxaaTrak / bxaaTrik

- Give the names of your immediate family members, e.g. ism bayyi *lari (the name of my father is Larry) ism immi....etc.... .

- Name people around you using demonstratives; e.g. hayda *toni, (this is Toni) etc... .

Chapter Three
Dates & Numbers

In this chapter you will learn more useful
expressions related to social life. You will also
learn the days of the week, months, seasons,
cardinal and ordinal numbers.

The verbs conjugated in this chapter are:
keen, wuSil, bi'i, nbasaT.

DIALOGUE I

*Hayaat:	lHamdilla 9a-ssaleeme ya *lori, kiif keenit safritkun?
*lori:	nuʃkur Hamdik ya *Hayaat, keenit safra Tawiile, ta'riiban 9aʃr se9aat biTTiyyaara, bus nuʃkur *alla wSulna bi-ssaleeme.
*Hayaat:	aymta wSultu min Gayr ʃarr?
*lori:	wSulna 9a*bayruut yawm-lxamiis, ssee9a arb9a ba9d-DDuhr.
*Hayaat:	wkam yawm raH tib'u b*libneen?
*lori:	ʃi ʃahr ta'riiban. leezim nirja9 bi'eexir *tammuuz li'annuu-lmadeeris bitballiʃ binuSS *aab.
*Hayaat:	9aZiim, nʃalla btunbusTu hawn,wibtirja9u bi-ssaleeme.
*lori:	ʃukran ya *Hayaat

CULTURE & VOCABULARY

As indicated previously the name of God (*alla) is
included in many expressions used in the Middle East to
express faith in Him and submission to His will.

Since some people are superstitious, they also use the
name of God to protect babies and belongings from the
harm that may be caused by evil eyes. Expressions like

"sm*alla" which means (the name of God) are used when you see a newly born baby or you talk about someone's successful business or beautiful family etc... .

lHamdilla 9a-ssaleeme:	means lit. "praise God for you safety". It is used in this context as "welcome back". It is also used to wish someone a good recovery from an illness, surgery, or an accident.
keenit:	it was. Perf. of verb keen (to be). See grammar notes.
safritkun:	your trip. safra: trip. **The last vowel is dropped or modified when a pronominal suffix is connected to a feminine noun and the silent /t/ reappears.** safra should not be confused with Safra which means yellow (fem.).
Tawiile:	long (fem.), Tawiil (masc.).
ta'riiban:	almost, about, approximately.
9aʃr:	ten (when followed by a noun, otherwise 9aʃra).
se9aat:	hours, see9a (sing.).
Tiyyaara:	aircraft.
bas:	but.
wSulna:	we arrived. Perf. of wuSil (to arrive).
min Gayr ʃarr:	may you be protected from evil.

*bayruut: capital and largest city of Lebanon.

yawm: day.

xamiis   Thursday, not to be confused with
                xaamis (fifth).

see9a: hour, watch, clock, se9aat (pl.).

arb9a: four.

ba9d: after.

Duhr: noon.

tib'u: imperf. of bi'i (to stay, to remain).
                See grammar notes.

ʃi: about, around. **When it occurs at the end
                of a statement it is used as an interroga-
                tive particle and the statement becomes a
                question with a rise of intonation, e.g.
                wuSil ʃi?** (did he arrive?)

ʃahr: month, uʃhur (pl.).

leezim: it is a must, it is necessary, should.

nirja9:   we return, imperf. of riji9 (to return),
                conjugated like ʃirib in Chapter II.

eexir: end, last.

*tammuuz: July.

li'annu: because.

madeeris: schools, madrase (sing.).

bitballiʃ: imperf. of ballaʃ (to start, to begin), conju-
              gated like 9arraf in Chapter II.

nuSS: mid, half.

*aab: August.

9aZiim: great. Other expressions used in the
              course of a conversation: ktiir mniiH
              (very good); mumteez (excellent); tiHfe
              (fantastic); Tayyib (ok, lit., delicious).

btunbusTu: you have fun. Imperf. of nbasaT(to enjoy
              oneself, to have fun). See grammar notes.

hawn: here.

DIALOGUE II

*9iSaam: kam Saff 9indak lyawm ya *xaliil?
*xaliil: 9indi tleet Sfuuf.
*9iSaam: ayya see9a biballiʃ awwal Saff?
*xaliil: awwal Saff biballiʃ ssee9a tis9a wnuSS.
*9iSaam: wl'ayya see9a btib'a biljeem9a?
*xaliil: 9aadatan, birja9 9albayt ba9d eexir Saff,
              Haweele-ssee9a tnayn illa rib9, ba9d
              DDuhr.

CULTURE & VOCABULARY

kam: how much, how many.

Saff: class, course, Sfuuf (pl.)

9indak: you have. **The preposition 9ind followed by a pronominal suffix** denotes possession, it is the equivalent of verb: to have.

lyawm: today.

tleet: three. Originally **tleete.** It looses the /e/ before a noun.

ayya: which?

awwal: first.

tis9a: nine. It looses the /a/ before a noun.

jeem9a: university, jeem9aat (pl.).

9aadatan: usually.

bayt: house, byuut (pl.).

Haweele: around, about.

tnayn: two (speaking about time), otherwise the dual form ending "ayn" is used to denote two counts, e.g. baytayn: two houses.

illa: minus, less.

rib9:   quarter. "tnayn illa rib9" means: quarter till 2.

ba9d: after, more.

Duhr: noon.

GRAMMAR NOTES

• **keen (to be)** is a key verb in Arabic and in the leb. dialect. It is also used as a helping verb in past tenses. It is a hollow verb used as an example for the conjugation of many similar hollow verbs.

Pronoun	Perfect	Imperfect	Imperative
huwwe	keen	ykuun	
hiyyi	keenit	tkuun	
hinni	keenu	ykuunu	
inta	kint	tkuun	kuun
inti	kinti	tkuuni	kuuni
intu	kintu	tkuunu	kuunu
ana	kint	kuun	
niHna	kinna	nkuun	

Verbs conjugated like keen: **feet** (to enter), **raaH** (to go).

• **wuSil (to arrive)** is a Measure I assimilated verb.

Pronoun	Perfect	Imperfect	Imperative
huwwe	wuSil	yuuSal	
hiyyi	wuSlit	tuuSal	
hinni	wuSlu	yuuSalu	
inta	wSult	tuuSal	wSaal
inti	wSulti	tuuSali	wSali ·
intu	wSultu	TuuSalu	wSalu
ana	wSult	uuSal	
niHna	wSulna	nuuSal	

- **bi'i (to stay)** is a Measure I defective verb.

Pronoun	Perfect	Imperfect	Imperative
huwwe	bi'i	yib'a	
hiyyi	bi'yit	tib'a	
hinni	bi'yu	yib'u	
inta	b'iit	tib'a	b'aa
inti	b'iiti	tib'i	b'ii
intu	b'iitu	tib'u	b'uu
ana	b'iit	ib'a	
niHna	b'iina	nib'a	

- **nbasaT (to enjoy oneself)** is a Measure VII sound verb.

Pronoun	Perfect	Imperfect	Imperative
huwwe	nbasaT	yunbusiT	
hiyyi	nbasaTit	tunbusiT	
hinni	nbasaTu	yunbusTu	
inta	nbasaTet	tunbusiT	nbusiT
inti	nbasaTti	tunbusTi	nbusTi
intu	nbasaTtu	tunbusTu	nbusTu
ana	nbasaTet	unbusiT	
niHna	nbasaTna	nunbusiT	

OTHER USEFUL VOCABULARY

Cardinal numbers

one	waaHad (does not modify nouns, it only follows a noun for emphasis).

two	tnayn (does not modify nouns, use dual form instead as seen before).	
three	tleete	
four	arb9a	
five	xamse	Numbers 3 thru 10 are followed by the plural form of the noun they modify. They also lose their final vowel before that noun, e.g. xams byuut, 9aʃr se9aat.
six	sitte	
seven	sab9a	
eight	tmeene	
nine	tis9a	
ten	9aʃra	
eleven	Hda9ʃ	From 11 on, numbers are followed by the singular form of the noun they modify, e.g. 9iʃriin bayt.
twelve	tna9ʃ	
thirteen	tletta9ʃ	
fourteen	arba9ta9ʃ	
fifteen	xamsta9ʃ	From 11-19, numbers take /ar/ before the noun they modify, e.g. xamsta9ʃar bayt.
sixteen	sitta9ʃ	
seventeen	saba9ta9ʃ	
eighteen	tmenta9ʃ	
nineteen	tisa9ta9ʃ	
twenty	9iʃriin	
twenty one	waaHad w9iʃriin	
twenty two	tnayn w9iʃriin...	
thirty	tletiin	
thirty one	waaHad witletiin...	
forty	arb9iin	
fifty	xamsiin	
sixty	sittiin	
seventy	sab9iin	
eighty	tmeniin	
ninety	tis9iin	
hundred	miyyi	
hundred one	miyyi wwaaHad	
hundred two	miyyi witnayn	
two hundred	mitayn	
three hundred	tleet miyyi	
thousand	alf	

million	malyuun
billion	milyaar

Ordinal Numbers

first	awwal (masc.), uula (fem.)
second	teeni/teenye
third	teelit/teelte
fourth	raabi9 /raab9a
fifth	xeemis/xeemse
sixth	seedis /seedse
seventh	seebi9 /seeb9a
eighth	teemin/teemne
nineth	teesi9/tees9a
tenth	9eeʃir/9eeʃra
last	eexir

Ordinal numbers after tenth are not communly used, they are replaced by the word "ra'm" which means number, followed by a cardinal number after the singular form of the noun, e.g. "bayt ra'm Hda9ʃ", house number eleven, instead of the eleventh house.

Expressions related to numbers

quarter	rib9
half	nuSS
third	tilt
a little	ʃway
a lot	ktiir
minus	illa

Days of the week (ayyaam l'usbuu9)

day	yawm, nhaar
week	jim9a, usbuu9

Sunday	l'aHad
Monday	ttanayn
Tuesday	ttaleeta
Wednesday	l'urb9a
Thursday	lxamiis
Friday	ljim9a
Saturday	ssabt

Months of the year (aʃhur-ssini)

month	ʃahr
year	sini
January	kaanuun-tteeni
February	ʃbaaT
March	azaar
April	niseen
May	ayyaar
June	Hzayraan
July	tammuuz
August	aab
September	ayluul
October	tiʃriin-l'awwal
November	tiʃriin-tteeni
December	kanuun-l'awwal

The Seasons (alfuSuul)

Season	faSl
Winter	ʃʃiti
Spring	rrabii9
Summer	SSayf
Fall	lxariif

Expressions related to time

moment	laHZa
second	takki
minute	d'ii'a
now	halla'
later	ba9deen
today	lyawm
tomorrow	bukra
yesterday	mbeeriH
evening	9aʃiyyi, lmasa
night	layl
morning	SubH
noon	Duhr
weekend	wiikend

REINFORCEMENT

• Apply the numbers you learned on family members, e.g. I have three brothers, two sisters, five uncles....

• Give the names of family members using ordinal numbers, e.g. my first uncle is Jim, my second uncle is Robert....

• What are your favorite months & seasons?

• List briefly your activities for the day and give their times, e.g. 8:00 University (jeem9a),12:00 Lunch (Gada).....

• List your activities for the weekend.

LIBAN لبـنـان

100 L.L.

١٠٠ ايرا

MAY G. AL ACHKAR

Chapter Four
Post Office & Telephone

In this chapter you will learn how to conduct simple business at the post office and over the phone, as well as the necessary vocabulary to conduct such a business.

The verbs conjugated in this chapter are:
badd, ba9at, 9aTa, wazan, HaTT, Daa9, Hiki, 9alla, talfan, 9imil, 'eel, ttaSal, tikram.

DIALOGUE I

*saami:	ʃu ya *piter, lwayn raayiH?
*piter:	raayiH 9albariid, 9indi maktuub baddi ib9atu 9a *nyu york.
*saami:	maktuub t'iil amma xafiif?
*piter:	t'iil ʃway.
*saami:	iza t'iil, leezim ta9Tii la-mwaZZaf-lbariid, Hatta yuuzanu, wya9tiik wara' buul tHuTTun 9lay.
*piter:	kam yawm baddu la-yuuSal 9a*nyu york?
*saami:	Hasab. mumkin jim9a ta'riiban. 9ala kil Haal, iza-lmaktuub mhimm, b9atu msawkar, Hatta ma yDii9.

CULTURE & VOCABULARY

Postal and phone services in Lebanon are operated by government agencies. Recently cellular phone companies were authorized to operate in Lebanon and many people are using their services.

Mail boxes are not available in many areas, therefore, it is necessary to go to the post office (markaz-lbariid) in order to buy stamps, mail a letter, send a package, or even make a long distance or an overseas call, if there is no phone center (santraal) available in your area.

∫u ya:	what's happening? Informal interrogative used among friends. You may also hear "∫u yaba?" or "∫u fi ma fi?".
raayiH:	going, raayHa (fem.). Active participle (masc.) of verb raaH (to go), conjugated like keen in Chapter III.
bariid:	mail, post office.
9indi:	I have. The preposition "9ind" which means with, at, followed by the pronominal suffix "i".
maktuub:	letter, correspondence.
baddi:	I want, I need. **It is a helping verb conjugated only in the perfect tense and usually followed by the imperfect of another verb.** See grammar notes.
ib9atu:	I send it. Imperf. of ba9at (to send) followed by the pronominal suffix "u". See grammar notes.
t'iil:	heavy (masc.), t'iile (fem.). **The feminine of an adjective is formed by adding /e/ or /i/ to the masculine form, e.g. kbiir/ kbiire.**
amma:	or (conjunction used in interrogative forms) otherwise "aw" is used.
xafiif:	light weight, xafiife (fem.).

ʃway: a little bit. "ʃway ʃway" means: slowly.

ta9Tii: you give it. Imperf. of 9aTa (to give) fol-
             lowed by the pronominal suffix "i". See
             grammar notes.

mwaZZaf: employee, mwaZfiin (pl.).

Hatta: in order to, so that, until, even.

yuuzanu: he weighs it. Imperf. of wazan (to weigh)
             followed by the pronominal suffix "u". See
             grammar notes

wara' buul: stamps.

tHuTTun: you put them. Imperf. of HaTT (to put)
             followed by the pronominal suffix "un".
             See grammar notes.

9lay: on it. Prep. 9ala changes form when
             followed by pronominal suffix.

la-yuuSal: in order for it to arrive. When "la" precedes
             an imperf. verb it is a synonym of Hatta.
             yuuSal is the imperf. of wuSil, see
             Chapter III.

Hasab: it depends.

mumkin: may be, it is possible.

ta'riiban: almost, around, approximately.

9ala kil Haal: at any rate, anyhow.

iza: if.

mhimm: important, mhimmi (fem.).

msawkar: certified.

ma: not, **negative particle, it negates perf. &
                imperf. verbs.**

yDii9:   to be lost. Imperf. of Daa9 (to be lost). See
                grammar notes.

Dialogue II

*ʃarl:	alo, min faDlak fiyyi iHki ma9 *9ali?
*aHmad:	miʃ 9am bisma9ak mniiH, mumkin t9alli Sawtak?
*ʃarl:	xaweeja *9ali mawjuud?
*aHmad:	miin biriidu?
*ʃarl:	hawni SaaHbu *ʃarl, 9amtalfin min *london.
*aHmad:	ssayyid *9ali miʃ mawjuud halla', bitHibb titriklu xabar?
*ʃarl:	na9am, 9mul ma9ruuf 'illu yuttuSil fiyyi, bukra 9aʃiyyi 9almaktab.
*aHmad:	tikram ya sayyid *ʃarl.

Culture & Vocabulary

It is considered rude and impolite to call someone you do not know by his first name. Therefore, when you ask for someone over the phone you may use the following titles:

xaweeja, sayyid, isteez	•for men
sitt, madaam	•for women
madmozeel, demwazeel	•for miss or lady

min faDlak: if you please. Other expressions used: "iza bitriid" if you wish; "law samaHt" if you allow, or just "please".

fiyyi: may I? can I? It is a prepositional phrase formed by "fi" (in) and the pronominal suffix "i". Lit. it means: in me. It is usually followed by an imperf. verb.

iHki: I talk, I speak. Imperf. of Hiki (to talk). See grammar notes.

miʃ: not, a negative particle like "ma".

bisma9ak: I hear you. Imperf. of simi9 (to hear, to listen), followed by the pronominal suffix "ak". Conjugated like ʃirib, Chapter II.

t9alli: you raise. Imperf. of 9alla (to raise, to lift). See grammar notes.

Sawtak: your voice. You often hear this expression "9alli Sawtak" if the phone connection is bad.

mawjuud: present, available.

biriid: he wants. Imperf. of raad (to want). Conjugated like Daa9 in the grammar notes of this chapter. This verb is seldom used in the perf. tense, the auxiliary verb (keen) + the conjugated form of (badd) replace it, e. g. "keen baddu", "keen badda", "keen baddun" etc... .

SaaHbu: his friend. SaaHib (friend masc.) loses

the /i/ when connected to the following pronominal suffixes "u" and "i". aSHaab (pl.).

9amtalfin: I am calling. talfin is the imperf. of talfan (to call). See grammar notes.

titriklu: you leave for him. Imperf. of tarak (to leave). Conjugated like ʃakar, see Chapter II.

xabar: message, news. axbaar (pl.)

9muul ma9ruuf: do me a favor. 9muul is the imp. of 9imil (to do). ma9ruuf means favor, good deed. See grammar notes.

'illu: tell him. Imp. of 'eel (to say). The imp. changes form when connected to a pronominal suffix. See grammar notes.

yuttuSil: he contacts, he calls, he gets in touch. Imperf. of ttaSal (to call). See grammar notes.

tikram: with pleasure, I will oblige. Lit. for your sake, in your honor. **This verb is only used in the imp., tikram (masc.), tikrami (fem.), tikramu (pl.)**

GRAMMAR NOTES

In this chapter we covered a variety of Measure I, assimilated, hollow, and defective verbs. Each one has a particular conjugational pattern. We also covered some Measure II, and Measure VIII verbs. It is important that you understand the conjugational patterns of this chapter because it will often serve as a reference for future verbs.

Please remember that the prefix "9am" of imperf. verbs indicates that the action of such verbs is in progress. The prefix "raH" denotes the future.

• **badd (to want)** is an irregular verb conjugated only in the Imperfect.

Pronoun	Imperfect
huwwe	baddu
hiyyi	badda
hinni	baddun
inta	baddak
inti	baddik
intu	baddkun
ana	baddi
niHna	baddna

It is usually followed by the imperfect of another verb.

• **ba9at (to send)** is conjugated like ∫**akar** in the perf. tense only.

Pronoun	Perfect	Imperfect	Imperative
huwwe	ba9at	yib9at	
hiyyi	ba9atit	tib9at	
hinni	ba9atu	yib9atu	
inta	ba9att	tib9at	b9aat
inti	ba9atti	tib9ati	b9ati
intu	ba9attu	tib9atu	b9atu
ana	ba9att	ib9at	
niHna	ba9atna	nib9at	

• **9aTa (to give)** Emphasize long vowels when pron. suffixes are added.

Pronoun	Perfect	Imperfect	Imperative
huwwe	9aTa	ya9Ti	
hiyyi	9aTyit	ta9Ti	
hinni	9aTyu	ya9Tu	
inta	9Tayt	ta9Ti	9Ti
inti	9Tayti	ta9Ti	9Ti
intu	9Taytu	ta9Tu	9Tu
ana	9Tayt	a9Ti	
niHna	9Tayna	na9Ti	

• **wazan (to weigh)** is a Measure I assimilated verb.

Pronoun	Perfect	Imperfect	Imperative
huwwe	wazan	yuuzan	
hiyyi	wazanit	tuuzan	
hinni	wazanu	yuuzanu	
inta	wazant	tuuzan	wzaan
inti	wazanti	tuuzani	wzani
intu	wazantu	tuuzanu	wzanu
ana	wazant	uuzan	
nihna	wazanna	nuuzan	

• **HaTT (to put)** is a conjugated like **Habb** in the perf. but differs otherwise.

Pronoun	Perfect	Imperfect	Imperative
huwwe	HaTT	yHuTT	
hiyyi	HaTTit	tHuTT	
hinni	HaTTu	yHuTTu	

inta	HaTTayt	tHuTT	HuTT
inti	HaTTayti	tHuTTi	HuTTi
intu	HaTTaytu	tHuTTu	HuTTu
ana	HaTTayt	HuTT	
niHna	HaTTayna	nHuTT	

• **Daa9 (to be lost)** is a hollow verb but conjugated differently from **keen. The Imperative is not commonly used**.

Pronoun	Perfect	Imperfect	Imperative
huwwe	Daa9	yDii9	
hiyyi	Daa9it	tDii9	
hinni	Daa9u	yDii9u	
inta	Du9t	tDii9	Dii9
inti	Du9ti	tDii9i	Dii9i
intu	Du9tu	tDii9u	Dii9u
ana	Du9t	Dii9	
niHna	Du9na	nDii9	

• **Hiki (to talk)** is a defective verb.

Pronoun	Perfect	Imperfect	Imperative
huwwe	Hiki	yiHki	
hiyyi	Hikyit	tiHki	
hinni	Hikyu	yiHku	
inta	Hkiit	tiH	Hki
inti	Hkiiti	tiHki	Hki
intu	Hkiitu	tiHku	Hku
ana	Hkiit	iHki	
niHna	Hkiina	niHki	

• **9alla (to raise, to increase)**

Pronoun	Perfect	Imperfect	Imperative
huwwe	9alla	y9alli	
hiyyi	9allit	t9alli	
hinni	9allu	y9allu	
inta	9allayt	t9alli	9alli
inti	9allayti	t9alli	9alli
intu	9allaytu	t9allu	9allu
ana	9allayt	9alli	
niHna	9allayna	n9alli	

• **talfan (to call, to phone)** is integrated from French into the leb. dialect. It is conjugated like a quadriliteral sound verb.

Pronoun	Perfect	Imperfect	Imperative
huwwe	talfan	ytalfin	
hiyyi	talfanit	ttalfin	
hinni	talfanu	ytalfnu	
inta	talfant	ttalfin	talfin
inti	talfanti	ttalfni	talfni
intu	talfantu	ttalfnu	talfnu
ana	talfant	talfin	
niHna	talfanna	ntalfin	

• **9imil (to do, to make)** is a very common verb, used in different contexts.

Pronoun	Perfect	Imperfect	Imperative
huwwe	9imil	ya9mil	
hiyyi	9imlit	ta9mil	
hinni	9imlu	ya9mlu	
inta	9milt	ta9mil	9mul
inti	9milti	ta9mli	9mili
intu	9miltu	ta9mlu	9milu
ana	9milt	a9mil	
niHna	9milna	na9mil	

• **'eel (to say)** is a hollow verb conjugated like keen. The glottal stop may cause some difficulty. Do not confuse between (ilna, for us) & ('ilna, we said).

Pronoun	Perfect	Imperfect	Imperative
huwwe	'eel	y'uul	
hiyyi	'eelit	t'uul	
hinni	'eelu	y'uulu	
inta	'ilt	t'uul	'uul
inyi	'ilti	t'uuli	'uuli
intu	'iltu	t'uulu	'uulu
ana	'ilt	'uul	
niHna	'ilna	n'uul	

• **ttaSal (to call, to get in touch)** is a Measure VIII verb.

Pronoun	Perfect	Imperfect	Imperative
huwwe	ttaSal	yuttuSil	
hiyyi	ttaSalit	tuttuSil	
hinni	ttaSalu	yuttuSlu	

inta	ttaSalt	tuttuSil	ttuSil
inti	ttaSalti	tuttuSli	ttuSli
intu	ttaSaltu	tuttuSlu	ttuSlu
ana	ttaSalt	uttuSil	
niHna	ttaSalna	nuttuSil	

OTHER USEFUL VOCABULARY

At the post office

address	9inween
envelope	mGallaf
mailbox	Sanduu'-lbariid
package	pakee, Tard
postcard	kart postaal
scale	mizeen
value	'iime
weigh	wazn

On the phone

line	xaTT
busy	maʃGuul
to dial	Talab-rra'm
to hang up	sakkar-lxaTT, Tabaʃ-ssimmee9a
operator	santralist
phone call	muxaabara
public phone	heetif 9muumi
to pick up receiver	rafa9-ssimmee9a
telephone book	daliil-lhaatif
static	tiʃwiiʃ

REINFORCEMENT

• Ask someone to tell you where the post office is located.

• Ask the post office employee the following:
   1. how many stamps do I need to send this letter to the USA?
   2. how long would it take for the letter to arrive?
   3. how much does it cost to send it certified?

• Ask someone where you could make a phone call.

• Ask how much does a phone call to the USA cost.

• Tell someone: the line is busy.

• Leave a message with your name, your phone number, and the time you called.

Chapter Five
**Biographical Information
& Means of Transportation**

In this chapter you will learn how to give biographical information and talk about different means of transportation .

The verbs conjugated in this chapter are:
ʃtaGal, ija, maDDa, 'idir, axad, ʃaaraT, sta9mal.

Dialogue I

This dialogue is between a public safety officer (mwaZZaf-l'amn-l9aam) at the airport and *viktor.

mwaZZaf-l'amn-l9aam:	ʃu ismak?
*viktor:	ismi *viktor.
m:	ism-l9ayle?
*viktor:	*williams.
m:	'iddayʃ 9umrak?
*viktor:	9iʃriin sini.
m:	ʃu btiʃtiGil?
*viktor:	ana Taalib biljeem9a.
m:	hay awwal marra btiji 9a*libneen?
*viktor:	na9am, awwal marra.
m:	mnayn jeeyi?
*viktor:	min maTaar *ʃikago.
m:	ʃu raH ta9mil b*libneen?
*viktor:	jeeyi maDDi furSit-SSayf.
m:	ʃu 9inweenak b*libneen?
*viktor:	raH kuun seekin 9ind-ssayyid *xaliil *Sa9b, bineeyit *Harb, *b9abda.
m:	ʃukran, tfaDDal hayda pasporak. leezim truuH halla' 9ind mwaZZaf-ljamaarik. nʃalla btunbusiT b*libneen.

Culture & Vocabulary

When you arrive to Beirut International Airport, you have to pass by a Public Safety officer who will verify your passport and ask you security questions. After that, you will pick up your luggage or ask a porter to help you out, clear the customs (jamaarik) where you have to declare the value of the goods your are bringing with you and pay the related fees if required. If you are not a Lebanese citizen you need a visa to travel to Lebanon.

9umr: age. "idday∫ 9umrak?" (how old are you?). Sometimes the expression "taariix-lwilaade" (date of birth) is used instead.

bti∫tiGil: you work (masc. sing). Imperf. of ∫taGal (to work, to function). It is a Measure VIII verb. See grammar notes.

Taalib: student, Tullaab (pl.), usually it denotes a university student. Some people do not make the distinction between Taliib and tilmiiz, (pupil).

jeem9a: university, league, jeem9aat (pl.). Do not confuse with jim9a (week).

marra: once, one time, marraat (pl.). awwal marra (first time).

btiji: you come. Imperf. of ija (to come, to arrive). See grammar notes.

mnayn: where from? Short form of "min wayn".

jeeyi: coming, arriving. Active participle of ija.

maTaar: airport. Noun of place derived from verb
             Taar (to fly).

maDDi: I spend (time). Imperf. of maDDa (to
             spend time, to stay). 'aDDa is a synonym
             of maDDa conjugated the same way.
             See grammar notes.

furSa: vacation, holiday, opportunity, furaS (pl.).

seekin: residing, living, dwelling. Active participle
             of sakan (to reside). Conjugated like ʃakar,
             Chapter II.

bineeyi: building, bineyeet (pl.). Since Beirut and
             its suburb are becoming overcrowded
             and the price of land is very high, people
             are now living in large appartment
             buildings (bineyeet) rather than in private
             houses.

*b9abda: a large suburb of Beirut where the Presi-
             dential Palace is located.

paspor: passport, pasporaat (pl.). The word
             "jawaaz safar" is also used.

tfaDDal: in this context means: please take.

truuH: you go. Imperf. of raaH (to go). See
             Chapter IV.

halla':   now. halla' halla' means: immediately.

jamaarik: customs. Sometimes pronounced gamaarik.

Dialogue II

*viktor:	daxlak ya *9afiif, kiif bi'dir ruuH min-lmaTaar 9a*b9abda?
*9afiif:	aHsan ʃi, xud taksi, bas ʃaarTu 9assi9r.
*viktor:	layʃ ma fi otobuseet ?
*9afiif:	mbala, fi otobuseet, bas ma bitruuH diGri 9a*b9abda, bteexdak 9a*bayruut bil'awwal.
*viktor:	wkiif bruuH min *bayruut lahuniik?
*9afiif:	fiik teexud serviis.
*viktor:	ma fi treneet b*libneen?
*9afiif:	mbala fi treneet, bas ma Hada byista9mila lassafar. aktar ʃi byista9mluha ma9-lkamyuuneet laʃaHn-lbDaa9a.

Culture & Vocabulary

There are two major railroads in Lebanon. One connects Beirut to North and South Lebanon, the other connects Beirut to Damascus, Syria. Several years ago the railroads were used for the transportation of passengers and goods. Now heavy trucks are slowly replacing the obsolete railroad system for the freight of merchandise, and people rely on buses and cars for ground transportations.

Within Beirut and its suburbs, people have a choice between buses, taxis, or "services".

The big buses are operated by the government. One could also find some small individually owned and operated buses that serve a certain area.

Taxis are available all over Lebanon and they will take you anywhere you like for an agreed-upon fee. They operate through an office.

"Services" are individually owned vehicles, licenced by the government and used to take passengers from one station to another city or town for a fixed fare. Five passengers

may ride in the "service". The "service" may be used as a
Taxi if you prenegotiate the fare with the driver.

daxlak: is an interpellation device, it is the
                   equivalent of the imperative (say) when
                   you call on someone. When daxl is not
                   followed by a vocative, it is used as an
                   interjection expressing dismay, beseeching,
                   or endearment.
                   e.g.   yi, daxlu!   • I care less about him
                   daxlak ya *alla!   • I beseech you Lord
                   daxlu ʃu mahDuum! • how nice he is

bi'dir: I can. Imperf. of 'idir (to be able). It is the
                   synonym of "fiyyi". See grammar notes.

aHsan: better. aHsan ʃi: the best thing, the best way.

xud: take. Imp. of axad (to take). It is a
                   hamzated verb. **Like all hamzated verbs it
                   looses the hamza in the imperative.** See
                   grammar notes.

taksi: taxi. Foreign word integrated into the
                   dialect.

ʃaarTu: negotiate the fare with him. Imp. of ʃaaraT
                   (to negotiate, to set conditions, to bet). See
                   grammar notes. Tips "baxʃiiʃ" are not ex-
                   pected by taxi drivers but are appreciated.

si9r: price, fare, rate. as9aar (pl.). Another word
                   used for taxi fare is: ti9riife.

otobuseet: buses. otobus (sing.). Foreign word
                   integrated into the leb. dialect.

mbala: yes. Affirmative answer to a negative
              question.

diGri: straight, directly, non-stop, straight
              ahead.

serviis: a small vehicle for public transportation.
              The serviis makes frequent stops to pick
              up or drop off passengers who share the
              ride.

treneet: trains. treen (sing.).

ma Hada: no one.

byista9mila: uses it. Imperf. of sta9mal (to use), a
              Measure X verb connected to pronominal
              suffix. See grammar notes.

safar: travel, trip.

aktar ʃi: most of all, mostly.

ʃaHn: freight, shipping, transportation of goods.

bDaa9a: goods, merchandise.

GRAMMAR NOTES

When a verb or an active participle modifies another
verb, the second verb should be in the imperfect tense,
e.g. baddu yirja9, jeeyi iʃrab 'ahwe.

The affirmative answer to a negative question is
"mbala", the negative answer is "la" or "la'" followed

sometimes by the negative form of the verb, e.g. ma bitHibb-l'ahwe? mbala; ma bitHibb-l'ahwe? la' ma bHibba.

- ∫taGal **(to work, to function)** is a Measure VIII verb.

Pronoun	Perfect	Imperfect	Imperative
huwwe	∫taGal	yi∫tiGil	
hiyyi	∫taGalit	ti∫tiGil	
hinni	∫taGalu	yi∫tiGlu	
inta	∫taGalt	ti∫tiGil	∫tiGil
inti	∫taGalti	ti∫tiGli	∫tiGli
intu	∫taGaltu	ti∫tiGlu	∫tiGlu
ana	∫taGalt	i∫tiGil	
niHna	∫taGalna	ni∫tiGil	

- **ija (to arrive, to come)** is a **hamzated** and an **irregular** verb. A hamzated verb begins with a hamza which is dropped in the imperative. The irregular verb changes roots and may not be conjugated in certain tenses.

Pronoun	Perfect	Imperfect	Imperative
huwwe	ija	yiji	
hiyyi	ijit	tiji	
hinni	iju	yiju	
inta	jiit	tiji	ta9a
inti	jiiti	tiji	ta9i
intu	jiitu	tiju	ta9u
ana	jiit	iji	
niHna	jiina	niji	

• **maDDa and 'aDDa (to spend time, to stay)** have the same conjugation.

Pronoun	Perfect	Imperfect	Imperative
huwwe	maDDa	ymaDDi	
hiyyi	maDDit	tmaDDi	
hinni	maDDu	ymaDDu	
inta	maDDayt	tmaDDi	maDDi
inti	maDDayti	tmaDDi	maDDi
intu	maDDaytu	tmaDDu	maDDu
ana	maDDayt	maDDi	
niHna	maDDayna	nmaDDi	

• **'idir (to be able)** is not a hamzated verb. Its first letter /Q/ is pronounced as a glottal stop. **The prep. fi + pron. suffix is synonym to 'idir in the imperf. . To form the perf. you add verb keen to fi + pron. suffix.**

Pronoun	Perfect	Imperfect	Imperative
huwwe	'idir	yi'dir	
hiyyi	'idrit	ti'dir	
hinni	'idru	yi'dru	
inta	'dirt	ti'dir	'dur
inti	'dirti	ti'dri	'diri
intu	'dirtu	ti'dru	'diru
ana	'dirt	'i'dir	
niHna	'dirna	ni'dir	

• **axad (to take)** is a hamzated verb, it looses the hamza in the imperative.

Pronoun	Perfect	Imperfect	Imperative
huwwe	axad	yeexud	
hiyyi	axadit	teexud	
hinni	axadu	yeexdu	
inta	axadt	teexud	xud
inti	axadti	teexdi	xidi
intu	axadtu	teexdu	xidu
ana	axadt	eexud	
niHna	axadna	neexud	

• ʃaaraT (to negotiate, to bet, to set conditions) is a Measure III verb.

Pronoun	Perfect	Imperfect	Imperative
huwwe	ʃaaraT	yʃaariT	
hiyyi	ʃaaraTit	tʃaariT	
hinni	ʃaaraTu	yʃaarTu	
inta	ʃaraTt	tʃaariT	ʃaariT
inti	ʃaaraTti	tʃaarTi	ʃaarTi
intu	ʃaaraTtu	tʃaarTu	ʃaarTu
ana	ʃaaraTt	ʃaariT	
niHna	ʃaaraTna	nʃaariT	

• sta9mal (to use) is a Measure X verb derived from 9imil (to do), Chap. IV.

Pronoun	Perfect	Imperfect	Imperative
huwwe	sta9mal	yista9mil	
hiyyi	sta9malit	tista9mil	
hinni	sta9malu	yista9mlu	

inta	sta9malt	tista9mil	sta9mil
inti	sta9malti	tista9mli	sta9mli
intu	sta9maltu	tista9mlu	sta9mlu

ana	sta9malt	ista9mil
niHna	sta9malna	nista9mil

Other verbs conjugated like sta9mal:
  sta'bal: to welcome, to receive
  sta'jar: to rent
  staxdam: to use, to employ

OTHER USEFUL VOCABULARY

Biography

identity	hawiyye
height	Tuul
tall	Tawiil, Tawiile (fem.)
short	'aSiir, 'aSiire (fem.)
single	a9zab, 9azbe (fem.)
married	mjawwaz, mjawwze (fem.)
divorced	mTalla', mTall'a (fem.)
white	abyaD, bayDa (fem.)
black	aswad, sawda (fem.)
blond	aʃ'ar, ʃa'ra (fem.)
brown	asmar, samra (fem.) olive skin
profession	mihni, waZiife
educated	mit9allim
address	9inween

Christian	masiiHi
Maronite	maruuni
Moslem	mislim
Sunni	sinni

Shiite	ʃii9i
Druze	dirzi
Jewish	yehuudi

Means of Transportation

road	Tarii'
sea	baHr
air, space	jaww, faDa
land	arD, barr
wind	hawa
boat	markab, babor, beexra
small boat	ʃaxtuura
aircraft	Tiyyaara
passenger	reekib, rikkeeb (pl.)
seat	ma'9ad, ma'ee9id (pl.)
line, route	xaT, xTuuT (pl.)
ticket	tiket, biTaa'a, tazkara
porter	9itteel, 9itteele (pl.)
driver	ʃofœr
parking	parkin, maw'af
to drive	saa', ysuu' (imperf.)
road light	iʃaara, iʃaraat (pl.)
to pass	'aTa9, dawbal (it also means to repeat an academic year)
to beep	zammar (to beep the horn)
to brake	Darab freem
to stop	wa"af
door	beeb, bweeb (pl.)
window	ʃibbeek, ʃbebiik (pl.)
tire	duleeb, dweliib (pl.)
hitchiking	otostop
slow	baTii'
fast	sarii9

REINFORCEMENT

• Give a complete profile of yourself, of a friend or a family member. Include the following: name, age, color, marital status, education, address, etc...

• What is your favorite means of transportation? Why?

• What is the difference between "taksi" and "serviis"?

• Use the verbs of this chapter in meaningful sentences.

Chapter Six
Directions & Road Conditions

In this chapter you will learn how to ask for directions. You will also learn useful terms related to colors, traffic, and road conditions.

The verbs conjugated in this chapter are:
'aTa9, xaffaf, Tuli9, ntabah, sa'al, lee'a, 9irif, Dayya9.

DIALOGUE I

*joanna: min faDlak ya xaweeja, kiif fiyyi ruuH 9ala 'al9it *jbayl?

rrijjeel: awwal ʃi, leezim teexdi otostrad *Traablus, wtruuHi Sawb *juuni. ba9dma tu'Ta9i *juuni welkazino bʃi 9aʃr d'aayi', bitʃuufi mafra' *jbayl 9alyemiin.

*joanna: wba9deen, ʃu leezim a9mil?

rrijjeel: leezim txaffifi sayrik, wtuTla9i min-l'otostrad, wtinzali 9aʃʃmeel Sawb seeHit *jbayl. bas ntibhi, halla' fi 9aj'it sayr ktiir 9aTTarii'.

*joanna: lamma buSal 9ala seeHit *jbayl kiif bruuH?

rrijjeel: wa"fi 9ala mHaTTit benziin ws'ali, hinni bidilluuki.

CULTURE & VOCABULARY

In Lebanon there are two major highways: one links Beirut to the North and the South, it is a coastal highway along the Mediterranean Sea; the other links Beirut to Damascus and goes through the mountains of Lebanon and the Bekaa Valley.

Due to the overwhelming number of cars found on Lebanese soil one should expect traffic jams especially during rush hours and on roads undergoing repairs.

rijjeel: man, rjeel (pl.).

'al9a: fortress, 'lee9 (pl.). It becomes 'al9it when
                modified by another noun. Lebanon is
                known for its rich historical monuments
                and fortresses like the ones found in
                Baalbak, Sidon, Tripoli, Byblos, etc ... .

*jbayl: the historical town of Byblos, located
                about 40 miles north of Beirut.

awwal ʃi: first of all, when you are listing a
                sequence of events or words.

otostrad: highway, a foreign word integrated into
                the leb. dialect. It is understood that
                "otostrad" refers to the coastal highway.

Sawb: towards. When followed by expressions
                related to time, it means: around, e.g.
                Sawb ssee9a 9aʃra (around ten o'clock).

*juuni: a large city and port north of Beirut.

ba9dma: after, followed by a verb. ba9d means:
                after, ma introduces the verb.

tu'Ta9i: you pass, you cross. Imperf. of 'aTa9 (to
                pass, to cross, to cut). See grammar notes.

kazino: the famous "Casino du Liban" located
                in the area of *m9amiltayn, known for
                its luxurious gambling rooms and
                famous shows.

bʃi: approximately, around.

bitʃuufi: you will see. Imperfect of ʃeef (to see), conjugated like keen in Chapter III.

mafra':   exit, intersection, crossroad, mafaare'(pl.). It is a name of place derived from verb fara': to make a turn.

9alyemiin: to the right.

ba9deen: then, later, after.

txaffifi: you slow down. Imperf. of xaffaf (to slow down). Measure II verb. See grammar notes.

sayr: traffic. xaffifi sayrik: slow down, drive slowly.

tuTla9i: you exit. Imperf. of Tuli9 (to ascend, to go up, to leave, to exit, to rank). See grammar notes.

tinzali: you go down. Imperf. of nizil (to go down, to drop, to descend), conjugated like simi9, Chapter IV.

9aʃʃmeel: to the left. ʃmeel also means north. To distinguish betwee north and left some people use the word "yasaar" which means "left".

Hatta: until, so that, in order to.

seeHa: public square, open space, seHaat (pl.). It becomes seeHit when modified by a noun.

ntibhi:	be careful. Imp. of ntabah (to be careful or attentive). Measure VII verb. See grammar notes.

9aj'it sayr:	traffic jam.

Tarii':	road, way, Turu' (pl.).

lamma:	when.

wa"fi:	stop. Imp. of wa"af (to stop), conjugated like 9arraf in Chapter II.

s'ali:	ask. Imp. of sa'al (to ask, to inquire). See grammar notes.

9indi su'aal:	**I have a question.**

bidilluki:	they will direct you. Imperf. of dall (to show, to point, to guide), conjugated like Habb in Chapter II.

Dialogue II

*joanna:	bil'izn ya madaam, kiif biruuHu 9a markaz-lbaladiyye?
lmara:	kaffi diGri Hatta tuuSali Hadd-lfarmaʃiyya, bitfuuti biTarii' zGiiri 9aʃʃmeel, bi'aaxir-TTarii' bitlaa'i bank *bayruut. markaz-lbaladiyye wara-lbank.
*joanna:	wkiif ba9rif-lmarkaz?
lmara:	ma bitDayy9i abadan, bineeye bayDa, ʃbebiika xuDr, teeni Taabi', bitʃuufi-l'aarma w9alam *libneen faw'a.

Culture & Vocabulary

In many cities and towns in Lebanon street signs and house numbers are absent. Therefore, one should rely on landmarks or important sites to locate his destination. Such landmarks could be a church, a mosque, a bank, etc... In small towns, people are usually related and they know each other very well.

mara: woman, nisween (pl.).

bil'izn: excuse me, please, lit. with your permission.

markaz: center, headquarter, maraakiz (pl.).

baladiyye: municipality. markaz-lbaladiyye is the equivalent of City Hall.

kaffi: continue. Imp. of kaffa (to continue, to go on), conjugated like 9alla in Chapter IV. **Please note: bikaffi means " it is enough".**

diGri   straight ahead. **If it follows verb to speak or to say, it means "truth"**, e.g. Hiki ddiGri: he said the truth.

Hadd: near, next to, close to.

farmaʃiyya: pharmacy, drug store. Some people use the word Saydaliyye.

bitfuuti: you enter. Imperf. of feet (to enter), conjugated like keen in Chapter III.

zGiiri: small, narrow, zGiir (masc.).

eexir: end. When it modifies a noun it means:
                  the last.

bitlee'i: you find. Imperf. of lee'a (to find, to see,
                  to meet someone). See grammar notes.

wara: behind, in the back.

ba9rif: I know. Imperf. of 9irif (to know, to
                  recognize). See grammar notes.

bitDayy9i: you get lost. Imperf. of Dayya9 (to lose,
                  to get lost). Conjugated like 9arraf in
                  Chapter II.

abadan: never, at all.

bayDa: white, abyaD (masc.), biiD (pl.).

ʃbebiika: its windows, ʃibbeek (sing.).

xuDr: green (pl.), axDar (masc.), xaDra (fem.).

Taabi':   floor, level, story, Twaabi' (pl.).

aarma: sign, aarmaat (pl.).

9alam: flag, a9leem (pl.).

faw'a: on top of it.

GRAMMAR NOTES

• **'aTa9 (to cross, to cut, to pass)** The hamza is replacing
the /Q/.

Pronoun	Perfect	Imperfect	Imperative
huwwe	'aTa9	yu'Ta9	
hiyyi	'aTa9it	tu'Ta9	
hinni	'aTa9u	yu'Ta9u	
inta	'aTa9t	tu'Ta9	'Taa9
inti	'aTa9ti	tu'Ta9i	'Ta9i
intu	'aTa9tu	tu'Ta9u	'Ta9u
ana	'aTa9t	u'Ta9	
niHna	'aTa9na	nu'Ta9	

• **xaffaf (to slow down)** is a Measure II verb, similar to 9arraf with certain exceptions in the imperf. and the imperative.

Pronoun	Perfect	Imperfect	Imperative
huwwe	xaffaf	yxaffif	
hiyyi	xaffafit	txaffif	
hinni	xaffafu	yxaffifu	
inta	xaffaft	txaffif	xaffif
inti	xaffati	txaffifi	xaffifi
intu	xaffaftu	txaffifu	xaffifu
ana	xaffaft	xaffif	
niHna	xaffafna	nxaffif	

• **Tuli9 (to exit, to leave, to go up)**

Pronoun	Perfect	Imperfect	Imperative
huwwe	Tuli9	yuTla9	
hiyyi	Tul9it	tuTla9	
hinni	Tul9u	yuTla9u	

inta	Tlu9t	tuTla9	Tlaa9
inti	Tlu9ti	tuTla9i	Tla9i
intu	Tlu9tu	tuTla9u	Tla9u

ana	Tlu9t	uTla9
niHna	Tlu9na	nuTla9

• **ntabah (to be careful, to pay attention)** is a Measure VII verb.

Pronoun	Perfect	Imperfect	Imperative
huwwe	ntabah	yintibih	
hiyyi	ntabahit	tintibih	
hinni	ntabahu	yintibhu	
inta	ntabaht	tintibih	ntibih
inti	ntabahti	tintibhi	ntibhi
intu	ntabahtu	tintibhu	ntibhu
ana	ntabaht	intibih	
niHna	ntabahna	nintibih	

• **sa'al (to ask, to inquire)**

Pronoun	Perfect	Imperfect	Imperative
huwwe	sa'al	yis'al	
hiyyi	sa'alit	tis'al	
hinni	sa'alu	yis'alu	
inta	sa'alt	tis'al	s'aal
inti	sa'alti	tis'ali	s'ali
intu	sa'altu	tis'alu	s'alu
ana	sa'alt	is'al	
niHna	sa'alna	nis'al	

* **lee′a (to find, to see, to meet someone)** The hamza is replacing the /Q/.

Pronoun	Perfect	Imperfect	Imperative
huwwe	lee′a	ylee′i	
hiyyi	lee′it	tlee′i	
hinni	lee′u	ylee′u	
inta	lee′ayt	tlee′i	lee′i
inti	lee′ayti	tlee′i	lee′i
intu	lee′aytu	tlee′u	lee′u
ana	lee′ayt	lee′i	
niHna	lee′ayna	nlee′i	

* **9irif (to know, to recognize)** is a sound Measure I verb.

Pronoun	Perfect	Imperfect	Imperative
huwwe	9irif	ya9rif	
hiyyi	9irfit	ta9rif	
hinni	9irfu	ya9rfu	
inta	9rift	ta9rif	9raaf
inti	9rifti	ta9rfi	9rafi
intu	9riftu	ta9rfu	9rafu
ana	9rift	a9rif	
niHna	9rifna	na9rif	

* **Dayya9 (to lose, to get lost) is** not to be confused with **xisir: to lose money in business, investment, property, or in gambling.**

Pronoun	Perfect	Imperfect	Imperative
huwwe	Dayya9	yDayyi9	
hiyyi	Dayya9it	tDayyi9	
hinni	Dayya9u	yDayy9u	
inta	Dayya9t	tDayyi9	Dayyi9
inti	Dayya9ti	tDayy9i	Dayy9i
intu	Dayya9tu	tDayy9u	Dayy9u
ana	Dayya9t	Dayyi9	
niHna	Dayya9na	nDayyi9	

OTHER USEFUL VOCABULARY

Colors: Adjectives of color follow the noun they modify.

	masc.	**fem.**	**pl.**
white	abyaD	bayDa	biiD
black	aswad	sawda	suud
red	aHmar	Hamra	Humr
green	axDar	xaDra	xuDr
yellow	aSfar	Safra	Sufr
blue	azra'	zar'a	zir'
brown	binni	binniyyi	
beige	beej		
pink	zahr		
gray	rmeedi	rmeediyyi	
navy blue	kiHli	kiHliyyi	
orange	bird'aani		
violet	banafsaji		
gold	dihabi		
silver	fuDDi		

Directions

up	faw'
down	taHt
behind	wara, xalf
in front	iddeem
on	9ala
near	Hadd, janb
before	'abl
after	ba9d
far	b9iid
close	'ariib
inside	juwwa, inside something: bi'alb, e.g. bi'alb-lbayt: inside the house
outside	barra
here	hawn
there	huniik

Road Conditions

wide	9ariiD, 9ariiDa (fem.); weesi9, wees9a (fem.)
narrow	Dayyi', Dayy'a (fem.)
paved	mzaffat, mzaffatte (fem.)
empty	faaDe, faaDye (fem.)
hole	juura, juwar (pl.)
middle	nuSS
side	Taraf
slippery	bitzaHHit
icy	mjallad, mjallde (fem.)
clean	nDiif, nDiife (fem.)
dirty	mijwi, mijwiyye (fem.)
litter	zbeele
dangerous	xuTra

safe	eemne
check point	Heejiz
ticket	ZabT

REINFORCEMENT

• Give someone coming to see you precise directions on how to find your house.

• Look around you and locate a specific item using the vocabulary you learned.

• Compare the road conditions in a big city to the ones in a small town. City: madiine, town: madiine zGiire

• What are your favorite colors?

In this chapter you will become familiar with Lebanese food and cuisine. You will learn about customs and manners related to socializing when invited for a meal at someone's house.

The verbs conjugated in this chapter are:
faram, jeeb, amar.

DIALOGUE I

*huda:	masa-lxayr ya *layla, ʃu 9amta9mli?
*layla:	maʃGuuli lafaw' raasi. *saliim 9azam nees 9al9aʃa, wmiʃ 9aarfi ʃu baddi HaDDirlun.
*huda:	basiiTa, talfni 9almaT9am, w'uulilun yib9atulik ʃwayyit mezeet, w'inti 9mili ʃi SaHn ruzz 9adjeej, wjaaT salaTa ma9u.
*layla:	fikra 9aZiime, bus bfaDDil a9mil SaHn tabbuule, badl-ssalaTa. ʃu ra'yik?
*huda:	ʃu baddik bittabbuule, bteexud wa't ktiir, farm ba'duunis wbanaduura wbaSal, wma 9indik wa't lakil hal'iʃya.
*layla:	ma9ik Ha'. raH HuTT-ddjeej 9annaar, wtalfin la*saliim illu yjiib ʃi jaaT bi'leewa ma9u. yalla bxaatrik.
*huda:	ma9-ssaleeme.

CULTURE & VOCABULARY

If you are invited to a dinner party in Lebanon, you are not expected to arrive sharply on time. You may bring with you pastries, flowers (zhuur), or a bottle of alcoholic beverage if it is not religiously offensive to your host.

Exchanging kisses and hugs is not a common practice. It is only reserved for relatives and very close friends. In some conservative families, gender segregation is part of life and handshakes with women are prohibited.

Dinner starts usually after 8:00 and lasts several hours. People take short pauses between the courses of the meal. Music, songs, and dance may be a part of the dinner party.

maʃGuuli: busy, occupied, maʃGuul (masc.).

lafaw' raasi: up to my head, very busy.

9azam: to invite, conjugated like ʃakar in Chapter II.

nees: generic term for people, guests.

9aʃa: dinner.

miʃ: negative particle, usually precedes nouns, active participles, demonstratives, and prepositional phrases.

9aarfe: active participle fem. of 9irif (to know), 9aarif (masc.), 9aarfiin (pl.).

HaDDirlun: prepare for them. Imperf. of HaDDar (to prepare), conjugated like 9arraf in Chapter II. The /l/ that precedes the pronominal suffix /un/ is a preposition meaning: for. In this context, prepare means to cook (Tabax), conjugated like faram.

basiiTa: never mind, it is o.k., do not worry.

maT9am: restaurant, maTaa9im (pl.).

uulilun: tell them. Imp. of 'eel (to say). See
               Chapter III.

yib9atulik: they send to you. Imperf. of ba9at (to send).
               See Chapter IV.

ʃway: a little. ʃway ʃway means slowly. ʃwayyit
               is used before nouns.

mezeet: appetizers. The leb. cuisine is very famous
               for its rich and varied meeza which is a
               selection of many small dishes of appetizers.

SaHn: plate, dish, SHuun (pl.).

ruzz: rice.

djeej: chicken. ruzz 9adjeej is a famous dish.
               Cooked chicken is served over rice cooked
               with ground beef, pine nuts and almonds.

jaaT: big plate, juuT (pl.).

salaTa: green salad with lettuce, tomatoes,
               cucumbers, etc... .

fikra: idea, afkaar (pl.).

9aZiime: great, fantastic, 9aZiim (masc.).

bfaDDil: I prefer. Imperf. of faDDal (to prefer),
               conjugated like 9arraf in Chapter II.

tabbuule: the famous leb. salad, made with cracked
               wheat "burGul", tomatoes, parsley, onions,

lemon juice, olive oil, and spices. It is time consuming to prepare such a dish.

badl: instead.

ʃu ra'yik: what is your opinion? What do you think? ra'y means opinion.

ʃu baddik: what do you want? ʃu baddik b... means: leave .... aside, forget about... ʃu baddik bittabbuule: forget about tabbuule. You may review verb badd in Chapter IV.

wa't: time.

farm: chopping, cutting. Verbal noun of faram (to chop, to cut, to mince). See grammar notes.

ba'duunis: parsley.

banaduura: tomatoes.

baSal: onion.

iʃya: things, items, objects, ʃi (sing.).

ma9ik Ha':   you are right.

yjiib: he brings. Imperf. of jeeb (to bring). See grammar notes.

bi'leewa: famous Arabic pastry made with fillo dough, nuts, pistachios, and a rose water syrup called ('aTr).

DIALOGUE II

garson:	ahla wsahla, tfaDDalu.
rrijjeel:	baddi Taawle laʃaxSayn, Hadd-ʃʃibbeek iza mumkin.
garson:	tikram 9aynak. tfaDDalu,TTaawle HaaDra.
rrijjeel:	ʃu 9indak ʃi Taaza wTayyib lyawm?
garson:	fi kibbi, laHm miʃwi, kafta, ʃiiʃ Tawuu', wTab9an fi 9inna samak Taaza.
rrijjeel:	ʃu bitHibbi teekli ya 9ayni?
lmara:	Taali9 9abeele SaHn samak, ma9 Hummus wbaaba Gannuuj.
rrijjeel:	9mul ma9ruuf jiblna jaaT samak, wjaaT xuDra, wʃwayyit mezeet.
garson:	tikram 9aynak. ʃu bitHibbu tiʃrabu 9ara', aw biira?
rrijjeel:	jibla anniinit *pepsi lalmadaam, w'anniinit biira ili. w9mul ma9ruuf 9Tiina ʃi anniinit may, wmanfaDa zGiiri weHyeetak.
garson:	HaaDir, btu'mur ʃi Gayru?
rrijjeel:	la', saleemtak.

CULTURE & VOCABULARY

Although fast food restaurants like Pizza Hut and Kentucky Fried Chiken are becoming increasingly popular in Lebanon, traditional restaurants are still very attractive. One should count at least two hours for lunch and three hours for dinner in a gourmet restaurant.

Since it is not customary to go out for breakfast, people settle instead for a croissant, a thyme pie (man'uuʃi), a quick sandwich, or (ka9kit kneefe) a cheese based pastry stuffed in sesame seed bread.

Lunch and dinner begin with appetizers (meeza) followed by the main course which is usually grilled meat or poultry, game or fish, then fruits and pastry. Coffee is served at the end of the meal. Despite the fact that many people are becoming aware of the dangers of tobacco, smoking is not forbidden in restaurants. Some people take a cigarette break during their meal, others enjoy smoking a water pipe (argiile). You may discreetly ask your waiter to seat you away from smokers.

garson: waiter, from French "garçon", you may
             also use the word "maître".

Taawle: table, Taawleet (pl.).

ʃaxSayn: dual of ʃaxS, person, individual, aʃxaaS(pl.).

Hadd: near, close to.

ʃibbeek: window, ʃbebiik (pl.).

iza: if.

mumkin: possible.

tikram :   also (tikram 9aynak, or tikram 9aynik), is
             a courtesy expression that means literally
             "may your eye be honored". In this
             context it means: at your service, I am
             happy to oblige.

HaaDra: ready, HaaDir (masc.).

Taaza: fresh.

lyawm: today.

kibbi: famous Lebanese dish made with ground

meat, cracked wheat (burGul), chopped onions, pine nuts, and spices.

There are several kinds of kibbis:

kibbi nayyi:	raw kibbi
kibbi bilfurn:	baked kibbi
kibbit baTaaTa:	potato kibbi
kibbit la'Tiin:	pumpkin kibbi

laHm: meat, in general red meat.

miʃwi: grilled, from verb ʃiwi (to grill). Conjugated like Hiki in Chapter IV.

kafta: ground meet with minced parsley, chopped onions, and spices. It may be served raw, baked, or grilled on a skewer (ʃiiʃ kafta).

ʃiiʃ Tawuu': marinated chicken tenders grilled on a skewer.

Tab9an: of course.

samak: fish.

teekli: you eat. Imperf. of akal (to eat), conjugated like axad in Chapter V.

Taali9 9abeele: I feel like, I am craving for.

HummuS: garbanzo bean paste, with tahini sauce, lemon juice, olive oil, garlic, and spices.

babaGannuuj: baked eggplant, mashed with tahini sauce, lemon juice, olive oil, garlic, and spices.

xuDra: vegetables.

9ara':   the Lebanese national drink, similar to the
              Greek Ouzo, made out of grapes and anis
              seeds. It is a clear drink that turns milky
              white when mixed with water. It is served
              in small cups called "kees". When you
              drink to someone's health over a meal
              you say "keesak" or "keesik" or "keeskun",
              which means: to your health! Cheers!

biira: beer.

jibli: bring me, get me. Imp. of jeeb (to bring).
              See grammar notes.

annini: bottle, aneeni (pl.).

may: water. Although Lebanon is blessed with
              many fountains and rivers, people feel
              more comfortable drinking water inspected
              and bottled by private companies.

manfaDa: ashtray, manaafiD (pl.).

weHyeetak: by your life. It is a courtesy expression
              which usually means "please", "if you do
              not mind".

btu'mur: at your command. Imperf. of amar (to
              order, to command, to request).
              See grammar notes.

ʃi Gayru: anything else, something else.

saleemtak: your safety. In this context it means "nothing, thank you".

GRAMMAR NOTES

- **faram (to chop, to mince)** is a sound Measure I verb.

Pronoun	Perfect	Imperfect	Imperative
huwwe	faram	yufrum	
hiyyi	faramit	tufrum	
hinni	faramu	yufrmu	
inta	faramt	tufrum	frum
inti	faramti	tufrmi	frumi
intu	faramtu	tufrmu	frumu
ana	faramt	ufrum	
niHna	faramna	nufrum	

- **jeeb (to bring, to get)** is a Hollow verb.

Pronoun	Perfect	Imperfect	Imperative
huwwe	jeeb	yjiib	
hiyyi	jeebit	tjiib	
hinni	jeebu	yjiibu	
inta	jibt	tjiib	jiib
inti	jibti	tjiibi	jiibi
intu	jibtu	tjiibu	jiibu
ana	jibt	jiib	
niHna	jibna	njiib	

- **amar (to order, to command, to request)** is a
Hamzated verb.

Pronoun	Perfect	Imperfect	Imperative
huwwe	amar	yu'mur	
hiyyi	amarit	tu'mur	
hinni	amaru	yu'mru	
inta	amart	tu'mur	'mur
inti	amarti	tu'mri	'muri
intu	amartu	tu'mru	'muru
ana	amart	'u'mur	
niHna	amarna	nu'mur	

OTHER USEFUL VOCABULARY

Food. For an extended list of food items, please look
at the appendix.

Vegetables (xuDra)

artichoke	arDiʃʃawke
asparagus	halyuun
beans (green)	luubye xaDra
(kidney)	faSuulya
(lima)	faSuulya 9ariiDa
beet	ʃmandar
cabbage	malfuuf
carrot	jazar
cauliflower	arnabiiT
corn	dara
cucumber	xyaar
eggplant	batinjeen
leeks	sil'

lentils	9adas
lettuce	xass
onion	baSal
squash	kuusa
tomato	banaduura

Meats

beef	ba'ar
chicken	djeej
fish	samak
lamb	Ganam
veal	9ijl

Fruits

apple	tiffeeH
banana	mawz
cherry	karaz
fig	tiin
grape	9inab
lemon	laymuun HaamuD
orange	laymuun
plum	xawx
watermelon	baTTiix

Spices

garlic	tuum
mint	na9na9
mustard	xardal
parsley	ba'duunis
pepper	bhaar
salt	milH
sesame	simsum

Restaurant (maT9am)

ashtray	manfaDa
bread	xibz
chair	kirse
cup	finjeen
dish	SaHn
fork	ʃawke
glass	kibbeeye
knife	sikkiin
napkin	fuuTa
saltshaker	mamlaHa
spoon	mal9'a
table	Taawle
tablecloth	ʃarʃaf

Beverages

juice	9aSiir
lemonade	laymunaaDa
milk	Haliib
water	may
wine	nbiid

Personal Reactions

disgusted	'irfaan
full	ʃib9aan
hungry	juu9aan
starving	mxawwar
thirsty	9aTʃaan

REINFORCEMENT

- You are having friends over for dinner, what will you prepare for them?

• You are in a Lebanese restaurant ask the waiter about the daily special, then place an order.

• You notice that the fork and the knife are missing, bring that to the attention of your waiter.

• Ask your waiter to bring you the check (Hseeb)

In this chapter you will learn about clothing, apparel, fashion, fabrics, and other
related items.

The verbs conjugated in this chapter are:
libis, tlee'a, seefar, nisi.

DIALOGUE I

*amaal: *saamia 9azmitna 9ala 9urs binta bukra,
            w9ala Haflit-l'isti'beel. meHtaara ya
            *naadia ∫u baddi ilbus.
*naadia: walaw! xzeentik mitleene fsaTiin
            wtayyœraat. lay∫ ma btilbsi fusTaan
            l'aswad-TTawiil? Helu ktiir 9layki.
*amaal: fusTaan l'aswad Saar Dayyi' ∫way 9layyi,
            wma 9indi jizdeen yruuH ma9u.
*naadia: Tayyib, ∫u ra'yik bihayda-ttayyœr-lkiHli?
            modelu Helu, w9indik skarbini wjizdeen
            biruuHu ma9u.
*amaal: fikra 9aZiime. 9indi 9a'd, wjawz Hala'
            byilba'uulu ktiir, raH ilbisun ma9u. 9ala
            fikra, ayya see9a raH truuHi 9ind-
            lHillaa'?
*naadia: ma9i maw9ad-ssee9a tis9a wnuSS, baddi
            'uSS ∫a9ri wZabbTu ∫way.
*amaal: 9aal, ana ma9i maw9ad ma9u see9a
            9a∫ra. mnitlee'a huniik lakeen.

CULTURE & VOCABULARY

In general, Lebanese follow closely the latest styles
and fashions of European and Western designers. This is
the reason why many foreign expressions related to

clothing became integrated into the Lebanese dialect. The traditional Lebanese attire is only visible in some villages. Some Lebanese feel more comfortable wearing conservative clothing in accordance with their religious belief.

9urs: wedding

bukra: tomorrow

Hafle: party, celebration. Haflit l'isti'beel is the cocktail party or reception following the wedding. The word "cocktail" is also used.

meHtara: confused, puzzled, hesitant, meHtaar (masc.). It is derived from verb Htaar which means: to be confused, unable to choose.

ilbus: I wear. Imperf. of libis (to wear). See grammar notes.

walaw: interjection meaning: come on!

xzeene: closet, wardrobe, xzeneet (pl.).

mitleen: full, mitleene (fem.). One could also say (milyeen/milyeene).

fsaaTiin: dresses, fusTaan (sing.).

tayyœraat: ladies suits, tayyœr (sing.).

layʃ: why, also one may say (lay).

Tawiil: long, tall, Tawiile (fem.).

Helu: beautiful, nice, sweet, Hilwe (fem.).

9layki: on you, formed by the preposition 9ala
                    and the fem. pronominal suffix ki. The
                    preposition changes form if connected to
                    a pronominal suffix.

Saar: became, happened. Conjugated like Daa9
                    in Chapter IV.

Dayyi':   tight, narrow, Dayy'a (fem.).

ba9deen: furthermore, later.

jizdeen: purse, bag, jzediin (pl.).

yruuH ma9u: to match it, to go with it.

kiHli: navy blue, kiHliyyi (fem.).

model: style, fashion.

skarbiini: ladies shoes.

fikra: idea, thought, afkaar (pl.).

9a'd: neckless, 9'uud (pl.).

jawz: pair, husband.

Hala':   ear rings, Hal'a (sing.). Hala' also means:
                    to shave.

byilba':   it matches, it goes with. Imperf. of (libi')
                    to match, to go with, conjugated like riji9
                    in Chapter III.

9ala fikra: by the way.

Hillaa':   hairdresser, barber. The word "coiffeur"
            is also used.

maw9ad: appointment, mawa9iid (pl.).

'uSS: I cut. Imperf. of 'aSS (to cut), conjugated
         like HaTT in Chapter IV.

ZabbTu: I fix it. Imperf. of ZabbaT (to fix, to repair),
           conjugated like 9arraf in Chapter II.

mnitlee'a: we will meet. Imperf. of tlee'a (to meet, to
              run into). See grammar notes.

huniik: overthere.

lakeen: so, thus, therefore.

DIALOGUE II

*xaliil: ʃu ya *9iSaam, aymta msaafir 9a*nyuyork
            min Gayr ʃarr?
*9iSaam: ba9d yawmayn, iza *alla biriid. inta 9iʃt
            b*nyuyork, kiif-TTa's biʃʃiti huniik?
*xaliil: fi ktiir Sa'9a wtalj. ma tinsa teexud ma9ak
            kabbuut wʃamsiyye wtyeeb ʃatwiyye.
*9iSaam: Tab9an, raH eexud ma9i kameen kam
            kanzi wkalseet Suuf, wʃi SubbaaT xarj ttalj.
*xaliil: kam ʃanta eexid ma9ak?
*9iSaam: ʃanta wiHdi, ma bHibb Hammil GraaD
            ktiir.
*xaliil: xud ma9ak ʃi badle rasmiyye ma9 'amiiS
            bayDa wkravaat, barki n9azamt 9a ʃi Hafle.

*9iSaam: ma9ak Ha', ma9 innu ana bfaDDil ilbus
              bnaTliin w'umSaan spor,
              bas ma Hada bya9rif...
*xaliil: Tayyib, nʃalla bitruuH wibtirja9 bissaleeme.
*9iSaam: mamnuunak ya *xaliil.

CULTURE & VOCABULARY

mseefar: travelling. Active participle of seefar (to
                travel, to go on a trip). See grammar notes.

min Gayr ʃarr: lit. without evil. It is an idiomatic
                expression used to wish that the
                event will take place without any
                accidents or mishaps.

yawmayn: two days, dual of yawm.

iza *alla biriid: God willing.

9iʃt: you lived. Perf. of 9eeʃ (to live, to reside),
                conjugated like jeeb in Chapter VII.

Ta's: weather.

biʃʃiti: in the winter.

Sa'9a: cold, low temperature.

talj: snow.

ma tinsa: do not forget. **It is a negative command
                formed by the negation (ma) and the
                imperf. of verb nisi (to forget).**
                See grammar notes.

kabbuut: coat, kbabiit (pl). It also means "condom".

tyeeb: clothes.

ʃatwiyye: wintry, adj. related to ʃiti (winter).

kam: a few, (followed by a sing. noun) in an
                affirmative sentence. It means "how much,
                how many" in an interrogative sentence.

kanzi: sweater, kanzeet (pl.).

kalseet: socks.

Suuf: wool.

SubbaaT: shoe, SbabiiT (pl.).

xarj: suitable, good for, proper.

ʃanta: suitcase, ʃinat (pl.).

Hammil: I load up. Imperf. of Hammal (to load),
                conjugated like 9arraf in Chapter II.

GraaD: things, items, articles, GaraD (sing.).

rasmiyye: formal, serious.

'amiiS: shirt, 'umSaan (pl.).

kravaat: neck tie. From French "cravate".

barki: in case, may be, perhaps.

n9azamt: you were invited. From verb n9azam (to be

invited), conjugated like ntabah in
Chapter VI.

9a ∫i: to any given...., to a .... .

ma9 innu: despite the fact that.

bfaDDil: I prefer. Imperf. of faDDal (to prefer),
                   conjugated like 9arraf in Chapter II.

bnaaTliin: pants, trousers, bantalon (sing.).

spor: sport, relaxing.

ma Hada: no one. ma Hada bya9rif: no one knows,
                   no one can tell. Imperf. of 9irif (to know),
                   see grammar notes.

bissaleeme: with safety. May you have a safe trip.

GRAMMAR NOTES

• **libis (to wear, to put on)** is a sound Measure I verb.

Pronoun	Perfect	Imperfect	Imperative
huwwe	libis	yilbus	
hiyyi	libsit	tilbus	
hinni	libsu	yilbsu	
inta	lbist	tilbus	lbuus
inti	lbisti	tilbsi	lbisi
intu	lbistu	tilbsu	lbisu
ana	lbist	ilbus	
niHna	lbisna	nilbus	

• **tlee'a (to meet, to run into)** is a defective Measure VI verb. It takes a /y/ when connected to a pronominal suffix.

Pronoun	Perfect	Imperfect	Imperative
huwwe	tlee'a	yitlee'a	
hiyyi	tlee'it	titlee'a	
hinni	tlee'u	yitlee'u	
inta	tlee'ayt	titlee'i	tlee'a
inti	tlee'ayti	titlee'i	tlee'i
intu	tlee'aytu	titlee'u	tlee'u
ana	tlee'ayt	itlee'a	
niHna	tlee'ayna	nitlee'a	

• **seefar (to travel)** is a Measure III verb.

Pronoun	Perfect	Imperfect	Imperative
huwwe	seefar	yseefir	
hiyyi	seefarit	tseefir	
hinni	seefaru	yseefru	
inta	sefart	tseefir	seefir
inti	sefarti	tseefri	seefri
intu	sefartu	tseefru	seefru
ana	sefart	seefir	
niHna	sefarna	nseefir	

• **nisi (to forget)** is a defective Measure I verb.

Pronoun	Perfect	Imperfect	Imperative
huwwe	nisi	yinsa	
hiyyi	nisyit	tinsa	
hinni	nisyu	yinsu	
inta	nsiit	tinsa	nsa
inti	nsiiti	tinsi	nsi
intu	nsiitu	tinsu	nsu
ana	nsiit	insa	
niHna	nsiina	ninsa	

OTHER USEFUL VOCABULARY

Man's clothing

bathing suit	mayo
belt	'ʃaaT
boots	bot
bowtie	papiyon
briefs	sliip
gloves	kfuuf
handkerchief	maHrame
hat	burnaytTa
jacket	jakeet
jeans	jiinz
pajamas	pijaama
raincoat	tranʃkot
sandals	Sundaal
sneakers	spadri
suit	Ta'm
suspenders	bruteleet
T-shirt	tiʃert

tuxedo	smokin
undershirt	fanella
vest	Sudriyye
wallet	maHfZa

Woman's clothing

blouse	bluuze
bra	Sudriyye
change purse	jizdeen zGiir
coat	kabbuut
evening gown	fusTaan tawiil, fusTaan sahra
fur coat	kabbuut faru
pantyhose	kollan
scarf	iʃarp
shoes	skarbiine
skirt	tannuura
slip full	kombinezon
socks	kalseet
suit	tayyœr
underwear	kilot

Fabrics

cashmere	kaʃmiir
cotton	'uTun
flannel	fanella
gabardine	gavardiin
leather	jild
nylon	naylon
polyester	polyester
silk	Hariir
wool	Suuf

Sizes

big	kbiir
long	Tawiil
short	'aSiir
small	zGiir
tight	Dayyi'
wide	weesi9, 9ariiD

REINFORCEMENT

• Describe what you are wearing today.
Try to be specific and give fabrics and colors.

• Make a list of clothes you will take on your
next trip to Lebanon.

• What would you wear if you are invited to a
formal party?

• What would you wear if you are going
on a ski trip?

Chapter Nine
Health & Medical Problems

In this chapter you will learn about the human body and common health problems. You will also learn about some illnesses associated with travelling and living in a foreign country.

The verbs conjugated in this chapter are:
neem, wiji9, waSaf.

DIALOGUE I

*nawaal:	ʃu biki ya *kati? mbayyan 9layki te9beene, w9aynayki Humr.
*kati:	Sad'iini ya *nawaal, miʃ neeyme kil-llayl. 9indi waja9 raas, w9am bis9ul ktiir.
*nawaal:	axadti Haraartik ʃi?
*kati:	la'. bas Haassi inni maHruura ʃway, wkil jismi 9am yuja9ni.
*nawaal:	bi9ti'id ma9ik *griip. fi mawjit *griip bilbalad, wfi ktiir nees saaxne hal'iyyeem.
*kati:	ʃu ra'yik leezim a9mil? bruuH 9almistaʃfa?
*nawaal:	laa. l*griip ma baddu mistaʃfa. iza mitdeey'a ktiir, ruuHi 9ind-lHakiim barki byuuSuflik ʃi dawa wbitSiiri aHsan. saleemit 'albik.
*kati:	mersi ya *nawaal, *alla ysallmik.

CULTURE & VOCABULARY

It takes a serious illness for someone to see a doctor. Routine check ups are not yet very common, because Lebanon enjoys four distinct seasons, and in general people are healthy.

Medical care is the finest in the region because of the good quality of the Lebanese medical schools, and because most doctors and physicians are trained in Europe, the United States, and other well known medical schools in the world.

Private hospitals are thriving because many people are reluctant to seek medical help in public health facilities.

ʃu biki:	what is wrong with you? What is the matter with you?
mbayyan:	it looks, it seems, it appears. From verb bayyan (to appear), conjugated like 9arraf in Chapter II.
te9beene:	tired, te9been (masc.).
9aynayki:	your eyes, dual of 9ayn.
Sad'iini:	believe me. Imp. of Sadda' (to believe), conjugated like 9arraf in Chapter II.
neeyme:	sleeping. Active participle of neem (to sleep). See grammar notes.
kil:	all, the whole.
layl:	night, darkness.
waja9:	pain, ache, awjee9 (pl.).
raas:	head, ruus (pl.).
9am bis9ul:	I am coughing. Imperf. of sa9al (to

cough), conjugated like ʃakar in Chapter II. See Chapter III regarding use of **9am.**

Haraara:	temperature, fever.

Haasse:	I am feeling. Active participle of Hass (to feel), conjugated like Habb in Chapter II.

maHruura:	feverish, maHruur (masc.).

jism:	body, ajseem (pl.).

yuja9ni: is aching, is hurting. This is a very common expression associated with pain and ache. You add the part of the body that hurts to this expression in order to complain about the pain. If the part of the body is fem. the expression becomes tuja9ni; if it is plural: yuja9uuni. e.g. baTni 9am yuja9ni: my stomach is hurting , etc... .Imperf. of wiji9 (to hurt, to ache). See grammar notes.

bi9ti'id:	I believe, I think. Imperf. of 9ta'ad (to believe, to deem), conjugated like ʃtagal in Chapter V.

*griip:	flu, from French " la grippe".

mawje:	wave, epidemic.

balad:	country, bildeen (pl.).

nees:	people.

saaxne:	sick, saaxin (masc.).

mistaʃfa: hospital, mistaʃfayeet (pl.).

mitDaaya'a: not feeling well, bothered, annoyed,
                   mitDaaya' (masc.).

Hakiim: physician, M.D., wiseman. The word
                   doktœr is also used.

byuuSuflik: he will prescribe for you. Imperf. of waSaf
                   (to prescribe, to describe). See grammar
                   notes.

dawa: medication, idwye (pl.).

bitSiiri: you will become. Imperf. of Saar (to
                   become, to happen), conjugated like Daa9
                   in Chapter IV.

saleemit 'albik: lit. may your heart be safe. I hope
                   you feel better.

DIALOGUE II

*bernar: ʃu ya *9ali, ʃeeyfak 9am ti9ruj, ʃu-l'uSSa?
*9ali: Saar ma9i Haadis siyyaara mbeeriH
            9aTarii' *Sayda, bas lHamdilla ma Hada
            meet.
*bernar: miin keen fi ma9ak bissiyyaara?
*9ali: keen fi ma9i immi w'uxti. immi rawwaHit
            raasa ʃway, w'uxti jaraHit iida.
*bernar: ʃu 9miltu b9ad lHaadis?
*9ali: ijit siyyaarit l'is9aaf w'axaditna 9amistaʃfa
            *Sayda. Huniik Sawwaruula raasa
            la'immi, w'aTTabuula iida la'uxti.
*bernar: Tawwaltu bilmistaʃfa?

*9ali:	la' miʃ ktiir. b'iina ʃi see9a wnuSS biGurfit-TTawaari', wba9deen rji9na 9albayt.
*bernar:	lHamdilla 9assaleeme ya *9ali.
*9ali:	nuʃkur Hamdak ya axi.

Culture & Vocabulary

Foreigners may find driving in Lebanon very hazardous. One has to be very careful because roads are very congested and the speed limit is not always respected. Lebanese are known for their aggressive driving style. The completion of works on major highways and roads may solve the traffic problems and improve driving manners in the future.

Urgent medical care is available around the clock in private and public hospitals. Certain pharmacies, specially in large cities are open 24 hours. Ambulances are operated by the government, by private hospitals, or charitable organizations.

ʃeeyfak:	I see you. Active participle of ʃeef (to see, to notice), conjugated like keen.
ti9ruj:	you limp. Imperf. of 9araj (to limp), conjugated like ʃakar in Chapter II.
ʃu-l'uSSa:	what is the story? What's happening? 'uSSa: story, 'uSaS (pl.).
Saar ma9i:	I had, it happened to me.
Haadis:	accident, Haweedis (pl.).
siyyaara:	car, siyyaraat (pl.).

*Sayda: Sidon, a large historical city south of
             Beirut. It is known for its fortress, its port,
             and its Arabic pastries.

ma Hada: no one.

meet: to die, conjugated like keen in Chapter III.

rawwaH: to hurt, to be injured, conjugated like
             9arraf in Chapter II.

jaraH: to injure, to wound, conjugated like sa'al
             in Chapter VI.

iid: hand, idayn (dual), ayeede (pl.).

is9aaf: ambulance. The word "ambulance" is also
             used.

Sawwar: to x-ray, to take a picture, conjugated like
             9arraf in Chapter II.

'aTTab: to stitch, to sew, conjugated like 9arraf in
             Chapter II.

Tawwal: to stay too long, to lengthen, conjugated
             like 9arraf in Chapter II.

bi'i: to stay, to remain. See Chapter III.

GRAMMAR NOTES

• **neem (to sleep)** is a hollow verb.

Pronoun	Perfect	Imperfect	Imperative
huwwe	neem	yneem	
hiyyi	neemit	tneem	
hinni	neemu	yneemu	
inta	nimt	tneem	neem
inti	nimti	tneemi	neemi
intu	nimtu	tneemu	neemu
ana	nimt	neem	
niHna	nimna	nneem	

• **wiji9 (to ache, to be hurt)** is an assimilated verb. **It is usually associated with parts of the body.**

Pronoun	Perfect	Imperfect	Imperative
huwwe	wiji9	yuuja9	
hiyyi	wij9it	tuuja9	
hinni	wij9u	yuuja9u	
inta	wji9t	tuuja9	not applicable
inti	wji9ti	tuuja9i	
intu	wji9tu	tuuja9u	
ana	wji9t	'uuja9	
niHna	wji9na	nuuja9	

• **waSaf (to prescribe, to describe)** is an assimilated verb.

Pronoun	Perfect	Imperfect	Imperative
huwwe	waSaf	yuuSuf	
hiyyi	waSafit	tuuSuf	
hinni	waSafu	yuuSfu	

inta	waSaft	tuuSuf	wSuuf
inti	waSafti	tuuSfi	wSufi
intu	waSaftu	tuuSfu	wSufu

ana	waSaft	'uuSuf
niHna	waSafna	nuuSuf

OTHER USEFUL VOCABULARY

The Human Body (jism-l'inseen)

	Sing.	**Pl. (most common)**
ankle	keeHil	kweeHil
back	Dahr	
bladder	mabwale	
blood	damm	
body	jism	ajseem
bone	9aDme	9Daam
brain	nxaa9	nxa9aat
breast	Sudr	Sduura
cheek	xadd	xduud
chest	Sudr	
chin	da'n	d'uun
ear	dayne	dinayn
elbow	kuu9	kwee9
eye	9ayn	9yuun
face	wijj	wjeeh
finger	uSbi9	'Sabii9
foot	ijr	
gallbladder	mraara	
gum	niire	
hand	iid	ayeede
head	raas	ruus
heart	'alb	'luub

hip	wirk	wraak
jaw	fak	
joint	mafSal	mafaaSil
kidney	kilwe	kleewe
knee	rikbe	rikab
leg	faxd	fxaad
lip	ʃiffe	ʃfeef
liver	kibid	kbeed
lung	riyya	raweeya
mouth	timm	tmeem
muscle	9aDal	9aDalaat
nail	Dufr	Dafiir
neck	ra'be	r'eeb
nerve	9aSab	a9Saab
nose	munxaar	mnexiir
shoulder	kitf	kteef
skin	jild	jluud
stomach	baTn, mi9di	
throat	zle9iim, Hunjra	Haneejir
vein	9ir', ʃiryeen	9ruu', ʃrayiin

Commom Illnesses

blood pressure	DaGT (9aali: high; waaTi: low)
cold	raʃH
constipation	imseek, kteem
cough	sa9le
diarrhea	sheel
dizziness	dawxa
infection	iltiheeb
inflammation	waram
insomnia	'ala'
heartburn	Har'a
hemorrhage	naziif

Some Serious Illnesses

AIDS	sida
cancer	saraTaan
diabetes	sikkari
heart attack	kriiza bil'alb
jaundice	Sfayra
paralysis	ʃalal
tuberculosis	sill
ulcer	irHa

Some Handicaps

	Masc.	Fem.	Pl.
blind	a9ma	9amya	9imyeen
cross-eyed	aHwal	Hawla	Huul
crazy	axwat,	xawta,	xuut,
	majnuun	majnuune	mjeniin
deaf	aTraʃ	Tarʃa	Turʃ
lame	a9raj	9arja	9irj
mute	axras	xarsa	xirs
paralyzed	maʃluul	maʃluule	maʃluliin

Some Injuries

fracture	kisr
ligament sprain	falʃit 9ruu'
sprain	fikʃ

Vaccines (Tu9m)

measles	tʃiiʃi, HaSbi
mumps	buk9ayb
polio	ʃalal
smallpox	jidri

REINFORCEMENT

• You are in a pharmacy, ask the pharmacist for a medication for your headache and cough.

• You have the flu, describe to your doctor some of the symptoms associated with the flu.

• You were involved in a car accident, describe what happened and the injuries you have suffered.

• What are some of the common illnesses a foreigner may have when he/she visits a new country?

Chapter Ten
Professions & Careers

In this chapter you will learn about work, working conditions, professions, careers, as well as other related subjects.

The verbs conjugated in this chapter are:
Dall, ba9d (followed by a pronoun).

DIALOGUE I

*andre:	SabaaH-lxayr. lmhandis *Habiib mawjuud?
*Hasan:	la', ma9-l'asaf tarak 'abl ʃway, 9indu ʃuGl bilwarʃe lyawm.
*andre:	bta9rif ayya see9a raH yirja9?
*Hasan:	bi9ti'id ba9d-DDuhr. 9indu ijtimee9 ma9-lHiddeed, wnnijjaar, wssangari. wba9deen baddu yʃuuf lkihrabji wlbullaaT.
*andre:	mumkin itriklu xabar yuttuSil fiyyi lamma yirja9?
*Hasan:	tikram 9aynak, miin b'illu?
*andre:	lmuHaami *andre *matta min ʃirkit-DDamaan-lwaTani.
*Hasan:	tʃirrafna isteez *andre, lamma byirja9 l'isteez *Habiib bwaSSillu lxabar.

CULTURE & VOCABULARY

Traditionally, lawyers, physicians, engineers, and army officers were the favorite professions in Lebanon to the point that the market was glutted and Lebenese experienced shortness of skilled workers and labor. Thanks to many professional schools, young Lebanese have other options than going to universities and institutes of higher education.

mhandis: engineer, mhandsiin (pl.).

mawjuud: present, available, mawjuude (fem.).

ma9-l'asaf: with regrets, sorry.

tarak: to leave, conjugated like ∫akar in Chapter II.

∫uGl: work, business, employment.

war∫e: building site, working site, wira∫ (pl.).

ijtimee9   meeting, ijtime9aat (pl.).

Hiddeed: blacksmith, Hiddediin (pl.).

nijjaar: carpenter, nijjariin (pl.).

sangari: plumber, sangariyyi (pl.).

kihrabji: electrician, from kahraba: electricity. kihrabjiyyi (pl.).

bullaaT: floor tile layer, bullaTiin (pl.).

muHaami: lawyer, attorney, muHamiyyi (pl.)

∫irki: company, corporation, ∫irak (pl.).

Damaan: insurance, warranty.

waTani: national.

isteez: lit. means teacher. It is a title used to address educated people like professors, lawyers, and engineers.

bwaSSillu: I will convey to him, I will relate to him.
               From verb waSSal (to deliver, to convey),
               conjugated like 9arraf in Chapter II.

Dialogue II

*salma: ʃta'neelik ya *muna, wayn halGaybe?
*muna: bDall maʃGuule bilbayt wma9 luwleed.
*salma: wayn Saaru wleedik bilmadrasi?
*muna: likbiir, teelit sini jeem9a, 9am yitxaSSaS
            bi'idaarit-l'a9meel, witteeni, 9am yidrus
            muHaasabi.
*salma: wbintik-zzGiiri wayn Saarit?
*muna: ba9da bissaanawiyye, raH t'addim hassini
            9al*bakalorya nʃalla. w'inti, kiif 9ayltik?
*salma: killun mneeH lHamdilla. ibni likbiir 9am
            yidrus farmaʃeeni bikillyit-TTub, wbinti
            likbiiri 9am tidrus 9uluum siyasiyye
            biljeem9a-llibneeniyye, ba9d badda sini
            Hatta titxarraj.
*muna: w'ibnik-zzGiir, ʃu 9am yamil hal'iyyeem?
*salma: xallaS l*bakalorya wfeet 9alHarbiyyi,
            baddu ya9mil ZaabiT biljayʃ.
*muna: *alla yiHmii, wyxalliilik yaahun.
*salma: yxalli wleedik. Tayyib xallina nʃuufik.
*muna: tDalli bxayr.

Culture & Vocabulary

The Lebanese educational system is rated among the
best in the world. This is mainly due to bilingualism (Ara-
bic-English and Arabic-French), and to the stiff and rigor-
ous screening that students undergo from elementary
schools to universities. Every educated Lebanese speaks
at least two languages and has a knowledge of another.

The school curricula have to conform to the guidelines of
the Ministry of Education and to the recommendations of
the highly experienced pedagogues who work at the Educational Research Center.

wayn halGaybe: where have you been? Lit. where
                  was this absence?

Gaybe: absence.

bDall: I remain, I stay. Imperf. of Dall (to remain,
                  to stay). See grammar notes.

wleed: children, kids, walad (sing.).

madrasi: school, madeeris (pl.).

kbiir: old, big, kbaar (pl.).

sini: year, sniin (pl.).

yitxaSSaS: he specializes. Imperf. of txaSSaS (to
                  specialize, to study), conjugated like
                  tfaDDal in Chapter II.

idaarit-l'a9meel: business administration. idaara:
                  management, a9meel: business.

yidrus: he studies. Imperf. of daras (to study),
                  conjugated like ʃakar in Chapter II.

muHaasabe: accounting.

ba9da: she is still. When the preposition ba9d is
                  connected to a pronominal suffix it
                  conveys the meaning of verb **to be** + **still.**

saanawiyye: high school. Three years following the
middle school. At the end of the third year,
students will take the Baccalauréat exam.

t'addim 9ala: she takes an exam. Imerfect of 'addam 9ala
(to take an exam, to be a candidate). 'addam:
to present, to offer. Conjugated like 9arraf
in Chapter II.

hassini: **this year. ha or hal is a short demonstrative
used with masc. and fem. nouns.**

*bakaloria: official exam. given at the end of the last
high school year. Passing this exam. will
give students access to any university
that does not require an entrance exam.

9ayle: family, 9iyal (pl.).

farmaʃeeni: pharmacist. The word Saydali is also used.

killiyyi: college, faculty, school of higher education,
killiyyeet (pl.).

Tubb: medicine.

siyasiyye: political.

libneeniyyi: Lebanese, libneeni (masc.).

titxarraj: she graduates. Imperf. of txarraj (to gradu-
ate), conjugated like tfaDDal in Chapter II.

iyyeem: days, yawm (masc.).

xallaS: to finish, to complete, conjugated like
9arraf in Chapter II.

feet: to enter, to enroll, conjugated like keen in
                   Chapter III.

Harbiyyi: military academy where one graduates as
                   a commissioned officer. It is a prestigious
                   academy, admission is very competitive.

ZaabiT: officer, ZubbaaT (pl.).

jayʃ: army.

yiHmii: protect him. Imperf. of Himi (to protect),
                   conjugated like Hiki in Chapter IV.

tDalli bxayr: let's hope so. Lit. may you remain
                   in good health.

GRAMMAR NOTES

• **Dall (to remain, to stay)** is a doubled verb not to be
confused with **dall** (to point, to show, to indicate).

Pronoun	Perfect	Imperfect	Imperative
huwwe	Dall	yDall	
hiyyi	Dallit	tDall	
hinni	Dallu	yDallu	
inta	Dallayt	tDall	Dall
inti	Dallayti	tDalli	Dalli
intu	Dallaytu	tDallu	Dallu
ana	Dallayt	Dall	
niHna	Dallayna	nDall	

• **ba9d (after)** Preposition, behaves as a verb (to be still)

when connected to a pronominal suffix. It is conjugated
only in the Imperfect. In order to form the Perfect, the
conjugated form of verb **keen** in the Perfect tense
should precede it. The Imperative is not applicable.

Pronoun	Perfect	Imperfect
huwwe	keen ba9du	ba9du
hiyyi	keenit ba9da	ba9da
hinni	keenu ba9dun	ba9dun
inta	kint ba9dak	ba9dak
inti	kinti ba9dik	ba9dik
intu	kintu ba9dkun	ba9dkun
ana	kint ba9dni	ba9dni
niHna	kinna ba9dna	ba9dna

OTHER USEFUL VOCABULARY

Skilled workers

baker	furraan
butcher	laHHaam
barber	Hillee'
shoe repair	kindarji
taylor	xiyyaaT

Other professionals (miHtirfiin)

journalist	SaHaafi
nurse	mmarrid
physician	doktœr, Hakiim
pilot	Tiyyarji

Artists (finneniin)

artist	finneen
musician	musi'aar
painter	risseem
photographer	mSawwir
poet	ʃee9ir
sculptor	niHHaat
singer	mGanni, muTrib
writer	keetib

Politicians (siyasiyyi)

ambassador	safiir
consul	'unSul
deputy	neeyib
governor	Heekim, muHaafiZ
judge	'aaDi
mayor	muxtaar
minister	waziir
president	ra'iis

REINFORCEMENT

• Describe your educational background.

• What are the professions that require intensive training?

• Who are the skilled workers involved in building a house?

• Whom do you call upon if you have a problem with your plumbing system?

• What kind of arts do you appreciate? Why?

• Compare the educational system in your country, to the Lebanese educational system.

Chapter Eleven
Housing & Living Conditions

In this chapter you will learn about
housing, rentals, furniture, and other
related matters.

The verbs conjugated in this chapter are:
mara', beerak, farja, thanna, '9ad, ttafa'.

DIALOGUE I

*dunya:	min faDlak ya xaweeja, wayn bayt *kamaal *Tabbaal?
rrijjeel:	awwal bineeye 9alyamiin, wa"fi siyyaartik bilgaraaj, wTla9i bil'asansœr laTTaabi'-lxeemis, teeni beeb 9a∫∫meel.
*dunya	mamnuune. (ba9d ∫way)
*Hayaat:	ahla b*dunya, ∫u halmufeeja'a-lHilwe?
*dunya:	kint meer'a bilHay, Hibbayt beeriklik bi∫∫i"a-jjdiidi.
*Hayaat:	killik zaw', tfaDDali tafarjiiki 9albayt, bas ma tweexzina li'annu ba9dna 9am nifru∫, wilbayt naa'Su i∫ya ktiiri.
*dunya:	ba9rif, libyuut badda maSruuf ktiir, bas lwaaHad byifru∫ ma9u ma9u.
*Hayaat:	ma9ik Ha', tfaDDali min hawn. hayda-ddaar, whaydi 'uuDit-li'9uud. hawdi' uwaD-nnawm, kil 'uuDa ma9a Himmeema. haydi 'uuDit-ssufra,whawn-lmaTbax. hayda Himmeem laDDyuuf. wara-lmaTbax, fi 'uuDa zGiiri laSSaan9a. wmitl ma ∫eeyfe, fi balkoneet deeyir madaar. wfi kameen ∫ofaaj wmay suxni.
*dunya:	mabruuk, Helu ktiir halbayt, n∫alla btithannu fii.
*Hayaat:	∫ukran ya *dunya, yalla '9adi tani∫rab finjeen 'ahwe.

Culture & Vocabulary

It is not unusual for friends and family members to drop by and say Hi without calling ahead of time. It is recommended however to notify people or to call them before visiting with them.

Because Lebanon is a very small country (about 4015 square miles), land and housing are very expensive. The cost of living is also very high. This may be the reason why most people have difficulties buying and furnishing their new homes. Single homes are becoming very scarce in large cities and even in villages. People prefer to build apartments or large condominiums on their land and profit from their sale or rent.

bayt: house, home, byuut (pl.).

wa"fi: stop, park. Imp. of wa"af (to stop, to
                 park), conjugated like 9arraf in Chapter II.

garaaj   parking area, garage.

Tla9i: go up. Imp. of Tuli9 (to go up, to ascend,
                 to rank, to appear), conjugated like wuSil
                 in Chapter III.

asansœr: elevator, from French "ascenseur".

Taabi':   floor, story, level, Twaabi' (pl.).

beeb: door, bweeb (pl.).

ba9d ʃway: later on, after a little while.

mufeeja'a: surprise, mufeeja'eet (pl.).

meer'a: passing by, going by. Active participle of
               mara' (to go by). See grammar notes.

Hay: neighborhood, residential area, iHya (pl.).

beerik: from beerak (to congratulate, to bless).
               See grammar notes.

ʃi''a: large apartment or condominium, ʃi'a' (pl.).

jdiidi: new, recent, jdiid (masc.).

killik zaw':   you are so kind, so considerate. Lit. you
               are full of taste.

farjiiki: I show you. Imperf. of verb farja (to show).
               See grammar notes.

ma tweexzina: do not mind us, do not hold it against us.
               Negative Imp. of weexaz (to blame, to
               mind), conjugated like beerak in this
               chapter.

nifruʃ: we furnish. Imperf. faraʃ (to furnish),
               conjugated like ʃakar in Chapter II.

naa'Su: it needs, is missing.

iʃya: things, items, objects, ʃi (sing.)

maSruuf: expense, spending, mSariif (pl.).

waaHad: one, a person, an individual.

ma9u ma9u: little by little, slowly.

daar: living room.

'uuDa: room, 'uwad (pl.). 'udit li'9uud:
                family room.

nawm: sleeping, 'uwad-nnawm: bed rooms.

Himmeem: bathroom, Himmemeet (pl.).

'udit-ssufra: dining room.

maTbax: kitchen, maTaabix (pl.).

Dyuuf: guests, Dayf (sing.).

Saan9a: maid, servant, Sunnee9 (pl.).

mitl ma ʃeeyfe: as you can see. mitl: as, like; ʃeeyfe
                is the fem. active particple of verb
                ʃeef (to see), covered in Chapter VI.

balkoneet: balconies, from French "balcon".

deeyir madaar: all around, surrounding.

ʃofaaj: heating system, from French "chauffage".

may: water.

suxni: hot, suxn (masc.).

9aTuul: always, constantly, all the way.

btithannu: you find happiness, you enjoy. Imperf. of
                thanna (to find happiness, to enjoy), see
                grammar notes.

'9adi: sit down, have a seat. Imp. of 'a9ad (to sit,
                       to stay), see grammar notes.

Dialogue II

*william: marHaba ya m9allim, 9indkun ʃi'a'
                       mafruuʃe lal'ajaar?
naTuur: Tab9an, 9inna ʃi''a Hilwe biteeni Taabi',
                       bitHibb tʃuufa?
*william: iza ma fi iz9aaj.
naTuur: ma twaaxizna, l'asansœr miʃ meeʃi, li'annu-
                       lkahraba ma'Tuu9a. raH nuTla9 9addaraj.
*william: ma bihimm.
naTuur: hayda mifteeH beeb-lmadxal, tfaDDal fuut.
                       hayda-ssalon, fi Sofa kbiiri wfotœy. haydi
                       'uDit-ssufra, fiya Taawle wsit karaasi.
                       hawne 'uwaD-nnawm, kil 'uuDa fiya
                       taxtayn wxzeneet bilHayT.
*william: kam Himmeem fi?
naTuur: fi Himmeemayn,waaHad bayn 'uwaD-
                       nnawm witteeni Hadd-lmaTbax . hayda-
                       lmaTbax, fi birraad wfurn 9a-lGaaz, wfi
                       kameen Gisseele wniʃʃeefe. bihayda-jjaruur
                       fi dazziinit ʃuwak, wmlee9i', wskekiin.
                       9arraff, fi nuS dazziinit kibbeyeet, wSHuun,
                       wfnejiin 'ahwe.
*william: miin byidfa9-lkahraba, wlmay, wSSiyaani?
naTuur: hawdi 9almista'jir.
*william: 'iddayʃ ajaara haʃʃi''a?
naTuur: Saahib-lmilk Taalib arba9 miyyit dolaar
                       biʃʃahr, fiik tiHki ma9u.
*william: Tayyib, mamnuunak.

Culture & Vocabulary

The Lebanese civil war took its toll on the economy, and

the Lebanese pound (lira) which remained stable for a long time, finally collapsed. People trusted the U.S. $ more than any other currency to a point that all business trans- actions were negotiated in Dollars.

The Lebanese government has recently taken some steps to strengthen the Lebanese pound and ordered that all prices be posted in the national currency. The interest on deposits made in Lebanese pounds has also increased.

m9allim: lit. means teacher, skilled worker. It is
                 also used to address a person whose
                 name you do not know.

naTuur: janitor, concierge, nwaTiir (pl.).

mafruuʃe: furnished.

ajaar: rent.

Tab9an: of course.

iza mumkin: if possible.

miʃ meeʃi: not working, not functioning.

kahraba: electricity.

ma'Tuu9a: cut off, out of work.

nuTla9:   we go up, we ascend. Imperf. of Tuli9 (to
                 go up, to ascend), conjugated like wuSil
                 in Chapter III.

daraj: stairs, staircase.

ma bihimm: it does not matter, it is not important.

mifteeH: key, mfetiiH (pl.).

madxal: entrance, madeexil (pl.).

salon: living room. From French "salon".

sofa: sofa, couch.

fotœy: couch. From French "fauteuil".

Taawle: table, Tawleet (pl.).

karaasi: chairs, kirsi (sing.).

taxtayn: two beds, dual of taxt.

xzeneet: closets, xzeene (sing.).

HayT: wall, HiTaan (pl.).

bayn: between.

birraad: refrigerator.

furn: stove, oven.

9a-lGaaz: gas powered.

Gisseele: washer.

niʃʃeefe: dryer, not to confuse with seʃwaar: hair dryer.

dazzini: a dozen.

ʃuwak: forks, ʃawke (sing.).

mlee9i':   spoons, mal9'a (sing.).

skekiin: knives, sikkiin (sing.).

raff: shelf, rfuuf (pl.).

kibbeyeet: glasses, kibbeeye (sing.).

fnejiin: cups, finjeen (sing.).

byidfa9:   he pays. Imperf. of dafa9 (to pay), conju-
               gated like ba9at in Chapter IV.

Siyaane: maintenance.

mista'jir: tenant, mista'jriin (pl.).

SaaHib: owner, friend. SaaHib-lmilk: proprietor,
               owner. aSHaab (pl.).

tittifi':   you reach an agreement. Imperf. of ttafa'
               (to agree with, to get along, to reach an
               understanding), see grammar notes.

mamnuunak: thank you, I am grateful to you.

GRAMMAR NOTES

Some nouns ending with a vowel like 'uuDa, dazzini, etc... may change forms when they modify another noun. e.g. 'uuDit-nnawm (bed room); dazzinit ∫uwak (a dozen of forks).

In general the sound masc. pl. ending is **iin**, and the sound fem. pl. ending is **eet/aat.**

e.g. m9allim/m9allmiin; risseem/rissemiin,

mhandis/mhandsiin.
bint/baneet; 9amme/9ammeet; mmarDa/
mmarDeet.

- **mara' (to pass by, to go by)** is a sound Measure I
verb.

Pronoun	Perfect	Imperfect	Imperative
huwwe	mara'	yimru'	
hiyyi	mara'it	timru'	
hinni	mara'u	yimr'u	
inta	mara't	timru'	mru'
inti	mara'ti	timr'i	mri'i
intu	mara'tu	timr'u	mri'u
ana	mara't	imru'	
niHna	mara'na	nimru'	

- **beerak (to congratulate, to bless)** is a Measure III
verb.

Pronoun	Perfect	Imperfect	Imperative
huwwe	beerak	ybeerik	
hiyyi	beerakit	tbeerik	
hinni	beeraku	ybeerku	
inta	beerakt	tbeerik	beerik
inti	beerakti	tbeerki	beerki
intu	beeraktu	tbeerku	beerku
ana	beerakt	beerik	
niHna	beerakna	nbeerik	

• **farja (to show)** is a quadriliteral defective verb.

Pronoun	Perfect	Imperfect	Imperative
huwwe	farja	yfarji	
hiyyi	farjit	tfarji	
hinni	farju	yfarju	
inta	farjayt	tfarji	farji
inti	farjayti	tfarji	farji
intu	farjaytu	tfarju	farju
ana	farjayt	farji	
niHna	farjayna	nfarji	

• **thanna (to enjoy, to find happiness)** is a Measure V defective verb.

Pronoun	Perfect	Imperfect	Imperative
huwwe	thanna	yithanna	
hiyyi	thannit	tithanna	
hinni	thannu	yithannu	
inta	thannayt	tithanna	thanna
inti	thannayti	tithanni	thanni
intu	thannaytu	tithannu	thannu
ana	thannayt	ithanna	
niHna	thannayna	nithanna	

• **'a9ad (to sit down, to stay)** is a sound Measure I verb. The / ' / replaces the / Q /.

Pronoun	Perfect	Imperfect	Imperative
huwwe	'a9ad	yi'9ud	
hiyyi	'a9adit	ti'9ud	
hinni	'a9adu	yi'9du	
inta	'a9adt	ti'9ud	'9ud
inti	'a9adti	ti'9di	'9adi
intu	'a9adtu	ti'9du	'9adu
ana	'a9adt	i'9ud	
nihna	'a9adna	ni'9ud	

• **ttafa' (to agree with, to come to terms)** is a Measure VIII assimilitad verb.

Pronoun	Perfect	Imperfect	Imperative
huwwe	ttafa'	yittifi'	
hiyyi	ttafa'it	tittifi'	
hinni	ttafa'u	yittif'u	
inta	ttafa't	tittifi'	ttifi'
inti	ttafa'ti	tittif'i	ttif'i
intu	ttafa'tu	tittif'u	ttif'u
ana	ttafa't	ittifi'	
niHna	ttafa'na	nittifi'	

OTHER USEFUL VOCABULARY

The house

bell   jaras

ceiling	sa'f
concrete	baTon
darkness	9atm, Zalaam
entrance	madxal
floor	arD
garden	jnayne
inside	juwwa
light (noun)	Daw, nuur
light (verb)	Dawwa, walla9, ʃa99al
outside	barra
roof	saTH
stone	Hajar
window	ʃibbeek
wood	xaʃab

Appliances

dishwasher	jilleeye
freezer	tilleeje
microwave	mikro'ond
refrigerator	birraad
television	televizyon

Bedding

blanket	Hreem
comforter	lHeef
mattress	farʃe
pillow	mxadde
sheet	ʃarʃaf

The bathroom

bathtub	maGTas
bidet	bide

faucet	Hanafiyye
toilet	twaleet
toilet paper	wara' twaleet
toilet tank	sifon
towel	manʃafe
sink	maGsale

Cleaning tools

broom	miknse
brush	firʃeeye
bucket	dalu
mop	mamsHa
shovel	majruud
sponge	sfinje

REINFORCEMENT

- Describe your house.

- Would you like to live in a house or in an apartment? Why?

- In which room do you spend most of your time when you are home? Why?

- Based on the dialogue, compare rent in your country to rent in Lebanon.

- You would like to rent an apartment, gather as much information as possible about it before you sign the contract.

Chapter Twelve
Hobbies & Leisure Activities

In this chapter you will learn useful expressions related to hobbies and leisure activities. You will also learn about favorite sports, cultural activities, and night life in Lebanon.

The verbs conjugated in this chapter are:
t9aʃʃa, t'axxar.

DIALOGUE I

*Hamiid:	ʃu 9aamil hal wiikend ya *fawzi?
*fawzi:	iza-TTa's mniiH, 9am nfakkir nuTla9 9al*'arz na9mil ski. w'intu?
*Hamiid:	fi matʃ futbol bayn farii'-*nnijme wil*homenmen, bilmal9ab-lbaladi, ma9'uul nruuH nuHDaru.
*fawzi:	Tayyib ʃu ra'yak nruuH ba9deen nit9aʃʃa sawa, wnuHDar ʃi masraHiyye aw ʃi film?
*Hamiid:	min kill bid. ilna zameen ma HDurna masraHiyyeet. 9ala fikra, bi'uulu fi isti9raaD Helu lafir'it-lbalee-*rruusi bilkazino, bitHibb nruuH nuHDaru?
*fawzi:	marti bitHibb rra'S wilbalee, xalliini ʃuuf ʃu ra'ya, wbiHkiik-llayle.
*Hamiid:	bas ma tit'axxar ktiir, li'annu leezim talfin w'iHjuz, 'abl ma yruuHu-lmTaariH.
*fawzi:	wala yhimmak, bridd 9layk xabar bi'asra9 wa't.

CULTURE & VOCABULARY

Lebanese are by nature good-living fun-loving people. They love outdoor activities, especially outdoor restaurants and terraces. The mountains of Lebanon offer beautiful views of the Mediterranean.

Favorite sports in Lebanon are soccer, basketball, tennis, and volleyball. Lebanon is also a skiers, and swimmers' paradise. It is probably the only country in the world where in early Spring , you could water ski and within 20 to 30 minutes be on the ski slopes.

∫u 9aamil: what are your plans. 9aamil is the active participle of (9imil) to do, conjugated in Chapter IV.

nfakkir: we think. Imperf. of fakkar (to think), conjugated like 9arraf in Chapter II.

nuTla9:   we go up. Imperfect of Tuli9 (to go up, to ascend, to exit), conjugated in Chapter VI.

arz: cedars. In this context, it refers to the Cedar's area located in the mountains of North Lebanon, famous for its ancient cedar's forest and ski slopes.

mat∫:   game, match.

futbol: soccer, ball. American Football is not practiced in the Middle-East.

farii':   team, fira' (pl.).

*nijme: lit. star. The name of a Lebanese soccer team.

*homenmen: The name of a Lebnaese soccer team. Most of its players are from the Armenian-Lebanese community.

mal9ab: playground, field, stadium, malee9ib (pl.).

baladi: municipal.

ma9'uul: it is possible, conceivable, may be.

nuHDaru: we watch it. Imperf. of HuDir (to watch, to attend, to see), conjugated like Tuli9 in Chapter VI.

nit9aʃʃa: we have dinner. Imperf. of t9aʃʃa (to dine). See grammar notes.

sawa: together.

masraHiyye: theater play, masraHiyyeet (pl.).

film: movie, film, fluume (pl.).

min kil bid: by all means, definitely.

ilna zameen: it has been a while for us. ilna is formed by the preposition (ila) and the pronominal suffix (na). zameen: time.

9ala fikra: come to think about it, by the way.

fikra: thought, afkaar (pl.).

isti9raaD: a show, performance, isti9raDaat (pl.).

fir'a: group, ensemble, orchestra.

balee: ballet.

*ruusi: Russian.

kazino: Casino du Liban. See Chapter VI.

ra'S: dance.

llayle: tonight.

tit'axxar: you are late. Imperf. of t'axxar (to be
                 tardy, to be late). See grammar notes.

iHjuz: I reserve. Imperf. Hajaz (to reserve, to
                 book, to hold), conjugated like ʃakar in
                 Chapter II.

mTaariH: places, seats, maTraH (sing.).

wala yhimmak: don't you worry.

bridd xabar: lit. I will return a message. I will let you
               know, I will answer back. bridd is the
               Imperf. of radd (to return something),
               conjugated like Habb in Chapter II.

bi'asra9 wa't: lit. in the fastest time. As soon as
                 possible.

DIALOGUE II

*norma: ʃifti birneemij studio-lfann mbeeriH?
*riima: la', riHna 9a'oteel *karlton, keen fi ma9raD
             rasm wnaHt laTullaab killiyit-lfunuun,
             wrji9na m'axriin. layʃ, keen fi ʃi Helu?
*norma: ija ʃabb Sawtu mitl Sawt *wadii9-SSafi,
             Ganna wda' 9al9uud, kil-nnaas za"afitlu.
*riima: bisma9 innu halbirneemij maʃhuur ktiir, bas
             niHna bilbayt ma mnitfarraj deeyman
             9attelevizyon. ana bHibb-lmuTaala9a,
             wjawzi biHibb-rrasm.

*norma: kil waaHad 9indu hiwaaye bhalHayeet.
            ana bHibb-lmusii'a wil'aGaani-ʃʃa9biyye,
            wjawzi ma bihimmu illa-SSayd wli9b-
            lwara' ma9 aSHaabu.
*riima: ahamm ʃi, yi'dir-lwaaHad yGayyir jaw
            min wa't lawa't. law kil-lHayeet ʃuGl
            bʃuGl, keenu kil-nnees bimuutu min-lHaSr.

Culture & Vocabulary

Arts are highly appreciated in Lebanon. Art galleries, music recitals, poetry readings, and theatrical performances are very popular. There are several associations actively involved in encouraging and promoting Lebanese artifacts.

studio-lfann: Art Studio, a famous television show that encourages talented musicians, singers, and comedians. It offers them a chance to become stars.

oteel: hotel.

ma9raD: exhibition, ma9aariD (pl.).

rasm: painting.

naHt: sculpture.

killiyit-lfunuun: College of Fine Arts.

m'axxriin: we were late.

ʃabb: young man, ʃabeeb (pl.).

Sawt: voice, aSwaat (pl.).

mitl: similar, like.

*wadii9- SSaafi:	famous Lebanese singer. He played a major role in national folkloric festivals.
Ganna:	to sing, conjugated like 9alla in Chapter IV.
da″:	to play (an instrument), to knock on some thing, conjugated like Habb in Chapter II.
9uud:	oriental string instrument similar to the mandolin, stick.
za″af:	to clap hands, to applaud, conjugated like 9arraf in Chapter II.
maʃhuur:	famous, very well known.
mnitfarraj:	we look, we watch. Imperf. of tfarraj (to watch a program), conjugated like tfaDDal in Chapter II.
deeyman:	always, all the time.
muTaala9a:	reading for enjoyment.
kil waaHad:	every one, each one.
hiwaaye:	hobby.
Hayeet:	life.
musii′a:	music.
aGaani:	songs, Ginniyyi (sing.).
ʃa9biyyi:	popular, folkloric.
illa:	except.

Sayd: hunting, Sayd samak: fishing.

li9b: playing, game.

wara':   cards, papers, war'a (sing.).

ahamm ʃi: the most important thing.

yGayyir: he changes. Imperf. of Gayyar (to change), conjugated like 9arraf in Chapter II.

jaww: ambiance, atmosphere, climate.

min wa't lawa't: from time to time.

bimuutu: they die. Imperf. of meet (to die). See Chapter IX.

HaSr: stress, depression.

Grammar Notes

- **t9aʃʃa (to dine)** is a Measure V defective verb.

Pronoun	Perfect	Imperfect	Imperative
huwwe	t9aʃʃa	yit9aʃʃa	
hiyyi	t9aʃʃit	tit9aʃʃa	
hinni	t9aʃʃu	yit9aʃʃu	
inta	t9aʃʃayt	tit9aʃʃa	t9aʃʃa
inti	t9aʃʃayti	tit9aʃʃi	t9aʃʃi
intu	t9aʃʃaytu	tit9aʃʃu	t9aʃʃu
ana	t9aʃʃayt	it9aʃʃa	
niHna	t9aʃʃayna	nit9aʃʃa	

- **t'axxar (to be late)** is a Measure V verb.

Pronoun	Perfect	Imperfect	Imperative
huwwe	t'axxar	yit'axxar	
hiyyi	t'axxarit	tit'axxar	
hinni	t'axxaru	yit'axxaru	
inta	t'axxart	tit'axxar	t'axxar
inti	t'axxarti	tit'axxari	t'axxari
intu	t'axxartu	tit'axxaru	t'axxaru
ana	t'axxart	it'axxar	
niHna	t'axxarna	nit'axxar	

OTHER USEFUL VOCABULARY

Sports (riyaaDa)

basketball	basketbol, kurat-ssalla
boxing	muleekame, boks
game	matſ, mubaraat
golf	golf
judo	judo
karate	karate
ping pong	pinpon, kurat-TTaawle
skiing	ski
soccer	futbol, kurat-lQadam
swimming	sbeeHa
tennis	tenis, kurat-lmaDrib
volleyball	volibol, kurat- TTaa'ira
water ski	skinotiik, tazalluj 9almay
wrestling	muSaara9a
to win	ribiH
to loose	xisir
to be even	t9eedal

Hobbies (hiwayeet) & Leisure Activities (tasliye)

acting	timsiil
bike riding	rikb-lbisikleet
correspondence	mureesale
dancing	ra'S
drawing	tuSwiir, rasm
fishing	Sayd-ssamak
horsebackriding	rikb-lxayl
singing	Gina
stamps collecting	jam9 Tawaabi9
travelling	safar

Musical Instruments

accordeon	akkordeyon
flute	naay
guitare	gitaar
organ	org
piano	pyano
violin	vyolon, kamanja

REINFORCEMENT

• What are the most popular sports in your country?

• What is in your opinion the best exercice to stay in shape?

• What is your favorite pass-time? Why?

• Would you prefer to watch a movie or a theater play?

• Do you play any musical instrument? How often?

• Who is favorite singer? Why?

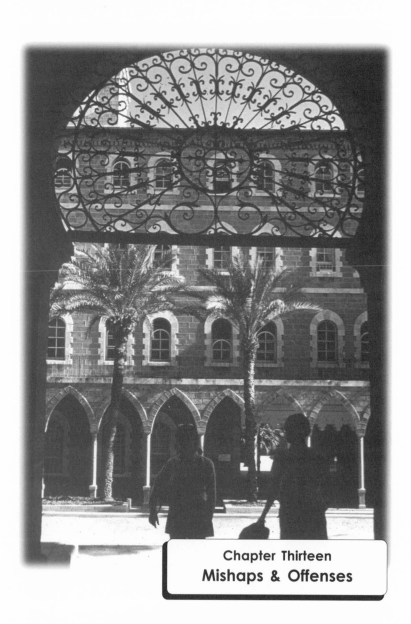

Chapter Thirteen
Mishaps & Offenses

In this chapter (which is coincidently
Chapter 13), you will learn useful vocabulary needed in times of emergencies,
offenses, or unforeseen circumstances.

The verbs conjugated in this chapter are:
xaaf, 9ili', and some incomplete verbs.

Dialogue I

*maryo: fiik t'illi ya *Gassaan ʃu hiyyi ba9D-
             lHaweedis-lmumkin tSiir ma9-l'inseen
             b*libneen?

*Gassaan: Tab9an. mitl kil balad, fi b*libneen
             Haweedis siyyaraat, wHaraayi',
             wjaraayim. laakin ijmeelan, lHaale-
             l'amniyye mniiHa, w'aHsan min Gayr
             bildeen.

*maryo: ʃu leezim ya9mil-lwaaHad iza Saar ma9u
             Haadis siyyaara?

*Gassan: iza fi jirHa, awwal ʃi leezim tuTlub-
             l'is9aaf, Hatta yeexdu-ljirHa 9almistaʃfa.
             teeni ʃi, leezim tuTlub xabiir Hatta yiji
             yikʃuf 9alHaadis wya9mil ti'riir.

*maryo: miʃ leezim nuTlub-lboliis?

*Gassaan: mbala, lakin 9adatan, lboliis ma biTawwil
             tayuHDar lamma bikuun fi Haadis
             mhimm

*maryo: mamnuunak, haydi ma9luumeet ktiir
             mhimmi. *alla yib9ud-lHaweedis.

Culture & Vocabulary

As we saw in Chapter IX, accidents are frequent in

Lebanon due to the overwhelming number of cars in the streets. When an accident occurs, it is important to call on a certified sworn expert (xabiir) to come to the scene and write a report on the accident. This report will be used by insurance companies and law enforcement officials to establish responsibilities. Every insurance company will provide you with a list of sworn experts.

ba9D: some.

inseen: human being, person.

Tab9an: of course, sure.

balad: country, bildeen (pl.).

Haraayi':   fires, Harii'a (sing.).

jaraayim: crimes, jariime (sing.).

laakin: but, however.

ijmeelan: in general.

Heele: situation, condition.

amniyye: safety, security.

aHsan: better.

jirHa: injured ones, wounded ones, jariiH (sing.).

xabiir: certified sworn expert, specialized in car accidents, xubara (pl.).

yikʃuf: he inspects, he looks at. Imperf. of kaʃaf 9ala (to inspect, to examine), conjugated like ʃakar in Chapter II.

ti'riir: report, file, ta'ariir (pl.).

boliis: police. Usually, the internal security
                    forces called "darak" are called upon in
                    case of accidents or crimes.

biTawwil: is late, takes time. Imperf. of Tawwal (to
                    be late), conjugated like 9arraf in Chapter II.

ma9lumeet: information.

yib9ud: he becomes distant. Imperf. of bi9id (to go
                    far, to become distant), conjugated like
                    libis in Chapter VIII.

*alla yib9ud-lHaweedis: may God prevent the occurance
                          of accidents.

DIALOGUE II

*yolanda: daxlik ya *jumana, layſ fi 9aalam ktiir
             Hadd halbineeye, bi'awwal-ſſeeri9 ?
*jumana: byiZhar innu fi Harii'a biTTaabi'-tteeni.
             ſeeyfi-ddaxne kiif 9am tuTla9 min
             Sawb-lbalkon?
*yolanda: ee, ma9ik Ha'. layki, layki, fi waaHad 9am
             bijarrib ynuTT min-ſſibbeek, bas hay'tu
             xeeyif li'annu-lmaseefe 9eelye.
*jumana: ana maTraHu, ma bxaaTir hayk. yaHHiyyi
             wuSlit-l'iTfa'iyyi.
*yolanda: ſu raH ya9mlu 'awltik?
*jumana: bi9ti'id raH yjarrbu yHuTTu sillum,
             wyxallSu-nnees halli 9il'aani juwwa,
             wba9deen biTaffu-lHarii'a.
*yolanda: ſu halwaZiife-lxuTra, nſalla ma Hada
             yxuSSu ſi.

Culture & Vocabulary

Fire hydrants are rare in Lebanon. In case of a fire, people and neighbors come very quickly to the rescue until the fire trucks arrive. Since all buildings and houses are made out of stones or concrete, it is easy to control a fire in its early stage, unless it is caused by a major explosion.

9aalam: people, crowd, world.

awwal: followed by a definite noun means: beginning; followed by an indefinite noun means: first.
              e.g. awwal-ʃʃeeri9: beginning of the street.
              awwal ʃeeri9: first street.

byiZhar: it seems, it looks. Imperf. of Zahar (to appear, to seem, to appear miraculously), conjugated like ba9at in Chapter IV.

ʃeeyfe: active participle fem. of ʃeef (to see), conjugated like keen in Chapter III.

daxne: smoke.

tuTla9:   it comes out. Imperf. of Tuli9 (to come up, to ascend). See Chapter VI.

layki: look, Imp. fem., layk (masc.). **It is not a conjugated verb.**

bijarrib: he tries. Imperf. of jarrab (to try, to attempt, to test), conjugated like 9arraf in Chapter II.

ynuTT: he jumps. Imperf. of naTT (to jump), conjugated like HaTT in Chapter IV.

hay'tu:

he seems. Expression made of hay'a (appearance) and a pron. suffix.

xeeyif:

afraid. Active participle of verb xaaf (to be afraid, to fear). See grammar notes.

maseefe:

distance, masefeet (pl.).

9eelye:

high, elevated, 9eele (masc.).

ana maTraHu:

if I were him, if I were in his place. maTraH: place, mTaariH (pl.).

bxaaTir:

I risk, I take a chance. Imperf. of xaaTar (to risk, to endanger), conjugated like ʃaaraT in Chapter V.

hayk:

like this, this way.

yaHHiyyi:

here it is, here she is. Invariable expression used with limited pronominal suffixes.
yaHHuwwi: here he is
yaHHinni: here they are (masc. or fem. pl.)

iTfa'iyyi:

fire fighters, fire trucks.

'awltik:

in your opinion (fem. sing.).

sillum:

ladder, sleelim (pl.).

yxallSu:

they save. Imperf. of xallaS (to save, to finish), conjugated like 9arraf in Chapter II.

9il'aani:

trapped, stuck. Adjective derived from verb 9ili' (to get cought, to be trapped). See grammar notes.

biTaffu: they extinguish. Imperf. of Taffa (to put
                  out, to extinguish), conjugated like 9alla
                  in Chapter IV.

ma Hada :   no one.

yxuSSu: lit. belongs to him. In this context ma Hada
                  yxuSSu ʃi: I hope to God no one gets hurt.

                  Imperf. of verb xaSS (to belong, to pertain),
                  conjugated like HaTT in Chapter IV.

GRAMMAR NOTES

Several expressions like **ba9d, daxl, hay'a, ka'an, layk, leezim, yaHHu,** etc...behave as incomplete verbs when connected to some pronominal suffixes. Some of them convey the imperative meaning; others the demonstrative, or the interpellation.

Although we have covered some of these expressions in previous chapters, it is useful to compare their meaning and their conjugational patterns.

Pronouns	ba9d (he is still)	daxl (say)	hay'a (to seem)	ka'an (as if to be)
huwwe	ba9du		hay'tu	ka'annu
hiyye	ba9da		hay'ita	ka'anna
hinni	ba9dun		hay'itun	ka'innun
inta	ba9dak	daxlak	hay'tak	ka'annak
inti	ba9dik	daxlik	hay'tik	ka'annik
intu	ba9dkun	daxlkun	hay'itkun	ka'ankun
ana	ba9dni		hay'ti	ka'anni
niHna	ba9dna		hay'itna	ka'anna

Pronouns	layk	leezim	yaHHu
	(watch, see)	(to need, to be a must)	(here it/he is)
huwwe		leezmu	yaHHu
hiyye		lezima	yaHHi
hinni		lezimun	yaHHinni
inta	layk	leezmak	
inti	layki	leezmik	
intu	layku	lezimkun	
ana		lezimni	
niHna		lezimna	

For a review of the different meanings of **daxl**, see Chapter V.

• **xaaf (to fear, to be afraid)** is a hollow Measure I verb.

Pronoun	Perfect	Imperfect	Imperative
huwwe	xaaf	yxaaf	
hiyyi	xaafit	txaaf	
hinni	xaafu	yxaafu	
inta	xift	txaaf	xaaf
inti	xifti	txaafi	xaafi
intu	xiftu	txaafu	xaafu
ana	xift	xaaf	
niHna	xifna	nxaaf	

• **9ili' (to get caught, to be stuck)** is a sound Measure I verb.

Pronoun	Perfect	Imperfect	Imperative
huwwe	9ili'	yi9la'	
hiyyi	9il'it	ti9la'	
hinni	9il'u	yi9la'u	
inta	9li't	ti9la'	9laa'
inti	9li'ti	ti9la'i	9la'i
intu	9li'tu	ti9la'u	9la'u
ana	9li't	i9la'	
niHna	9li'na	ni9la'	

OTHER USEFUL VOCABULARY

Crimes and misdemeanors (jaraayim, muxelafeet)

beating	Darb
fight	maʃkal, 9arke
kidnapping	xaTf
lying	kizb
murder	'atl, jariime
rape	iGtiSaab
theft	sir'a
threat	tihdiid
vandalism	tixriib

Criminals (mujrimiin)

crook	az9ar
criminal	mujrim
gang	9iSaabe
thief	sirree', Haraami

Justice (9adl)

court	maHkame
judge	'aaDi
lawyer	muHaami
witness	ʃeehid

Accidents (Haweedis)

damage	xaraab
drowning	Gara'
earthquake	hazze, zilzeel
flood	fayaDaan
war	Harb

REINFORCEMENTS

• What do you do if you have a car accident in Lebanon?

• Describe a car accident you had or witnessed.

• Who will respond to your call if you have a fire at home? What will they do?

• What are some of the crimes in your area?

• Describe a mishap that happened to you.

Chapter Fourteen
Nature & Climate

In this chapter you will learn useful vocabulary related to nature, climate, and weather conditions. You will become familiar with the different ways Lebanese spend their vacations.

The verbs conjugated in this chapter are:
zaar, 'arrar.

DIALOGUE I

*bill:	ʃu raH ta9mli bifurSit 9iid-l*mileed ya *lamya?
*lamya:	ili sintayn ma ʃift ahli, 9am fakkir seefir 9a*bayruut maDDi-lfurSa ma9un.
*bill:	niyyeelik, fiiki titsabbaHi wtʃimmi-lhawa kil-lwa't.
*lamya:	ma bi9ti'id raH i'dir itsabbaH ya *bill, li'annu-TTa's mis'i9 biʃʃiti bi*bayruut, wbtitluj biljabal.
*bill:	SaHiiH? ana kint mfakkar innu maneex *libneen SaHraawi, wma btitluj abadan bilmanTa'a 9indkun.
*lamya:	ma9-l'asaf, fi ktiir 9aalam eexde fikra GalaT 9an *libneen. lmaneex ktiir Helu. 9inna arba9 fSuul, wkil faSl aHla mintteeni.
*bill:	ana bisma9 innu balad raa'i9, wfi asaraat 'adiime, bas ma kint mfakkar innu maneexu Helu kameen. nʃalla bi'awwal furSa bi'dir ruuH zuuru.
*lamya:	ana akiide innak raH tunbusiT ktiir, xSuuSan iza bta9rif Hada huniik.

Culture & Vocabulary

Lebanon enjoys four distinct seasons. Each season has its beauty. Winter covers the mountains with snow. Spring brings back the aromas and perfumes of wild herbs and trees. Summer offers the swimmers and water skiers miles of blue Mediterranean water; the mountains are full with tourists and summer residents. Fall is a very picturesque and colorful natural painting.

furSa: vacation, break, holiday, opportunity, furaS (pl.).

9iid: feast, celebration, a9yeed (pl.).

mileed: birthday.

9iid-l*mileed: Christmas, celebrated on December 25.

In Lebanon there are several national and religious holidays such as:

9iid-l*'aDHa: the feast of immolation, celebrated on the 10th day of zu-lHijja of the Islamic calendar.
9iid-l*fiTr: the feast ending the Ramadan fast, celebrated the first of ∫awwal of the Islamic calendar.
ljim9a-l9aZiime: Good Friday
9iid-lkbiir: Easter
9iid-l'isti'leel: Independence Day, celebrated on the 22nd of November.
9iid-∫∫uhada: remembrance of the martyrs of World War I, celebrated on the 6th of May.

ili: it has been, it is mine. Prepositional phrase made
           of the preposition "ila" and pronominal suffixes,
           e.g. ili, ilak, ilik, ilna, etc... .If it denotes time (it
           has been) it is usually followed by the Perfect
           tense of the verb.

sintayn: two years, dual of sini.

ahli   my parents, my relatives.

seefir: I travel. Imperf. of seefar (to travel). See
           Chapter VIII.

niyyeelik: lucky you, good for you. Idiomatic ex-
           pression made of niyyeel and pronominal
           suffixes. e.g. niyyeelu, niyyeelak, etc... .

titsabbaHi: you swim. Imperf. of tsabbaH (to swim),
            conjugated like tfaDDal in Chapter II.

tʃimmi-lhawa: you have a good time, you travel for
              enjoyment. Idiomatic expression made
              of ʃamm (to smell, to breathe) conjugated
              like Habb in Chapter II, and the word
              hawa: air, wind.

miS'i9:   cold, also beerid.

faSl: season, chapter, fSuul (pl.).

jabal: mountain, jbeel (pl.).

SaHiiH: true, correct, right.

mfakkar: thinking. Active particple of fakkar (to
           think), like 9arraf in Chapter II.

maneex: climate.

SaHraawi: desert like. Adj. related to SaHra: desert.

manTa'a: region, area.

eexde: taking, having. Active participle of axad,
               conjugated in Chapter V.

GalaT: wrong, false, incorrect.

aHla: better.

raa'i9:   superb, marvelous.

asaraat: historical sites.

'adiime: ancient, old.

zuuru: I visit it. Imperf. of zaar (to visit). See
               grammar notes.

akiide: sure, certain, akiid (masc.).

xSuuSan: especially.

Hada: someone.

DIALOGUE II

*maha: byiZhar innu raH ykuun fi ʃawb wrTuube
               ktiir haSSayf, raH tDallu bi*Traablus aw
               raH tuTla9u 9a-ljabal?
*samar: Sadd'iini ba9d ma 'arrarna ʃu baddna
               na9mil. wleedna biHibbu yuTla9u 9aDDay9a,
               bas ana bi9tal hamm tuHDiir-lGraaD.

*maha:	kiif-TTa's biDDay9a?
*samar:	ktiir mniiH wSuHHi. aw'eet biSiir fi GTayTa SSubH, bas ba9deen btuTla9-ʃʃams, wfi bruud min 9aʃiyye.
*maha:	ma byuDjaru luwleed kil-SSayf?
*samar:	bil9aks, biDall fi Hafleet wsahraat bineedi-DDay9a, wibyil9abu kill-nnhaar ma9 wleed-ljiraan, w'aSHaabun, w'arayibun.
*maha:	la'ayya ʃahr bitDallu bi-ljabal?
*samar:	9aadatan Hatta eexir ʃahr ayluul. lamma yitGayyar-TTa's, wtsa"i9-ddini, ma bit9uud-SSayfiyye Hilwe.
*maha:	nʃalla btunbusTu, wtkuun Sayfiyye mniiHa.
*samar:	ʃukran ya *maha, tfaDDalu ʃarrfuuna.

CULTURE & VOCABULARY

Many Lebanese families have two homes, a winter home in a big coastal city (Beirut, Tripoli, Sidon, etc...), and a summer home in their hometown or a summer resort in the mountains. Few families are originally from Beirut. People enjoy spending the summer in their hometown where they can find their roots and be with their relatives.

ʃawb:	hot weather.
rTuube:	humidity.
*Traablus:	Tripoli, second largest city and port in Lebanon, located about 70 miles north of Beirut.
Sadd'iini:	believe me. Imp. of Sadda' (to believe), conjugated like 9arraf in Chapter II.

'arrarna: we decided. Perf. of 'arrar (to decide), see
               grammar notes.

Day9a: village, hometown, Diya9 (pl.).

bi9tal hamm: I worry, I feel distressed. Imperf. of 9itil
               hamm (to worry, to feel distressed). It is
               an idiomatic expression made of verb
               9itil, conjugated like ʃirib in Chapter II,
               and the word hamm: worry.

tuHDiir: preparation. Verbal noun of verb HaDDar
               (to prepare), conjugated like 9arraf in
               Chapter II.

GraaD: objects, things, items, odds and ends,
               GaraD (sing.).

SuHHi: healthy.

'aw'eet: sometimes.

GTayTa: fog, mist.

SubH: morning.

ʃams: sun.

bruud: cool breeze.

9aʃiyye: evening

yuDjaru: they get bored. Imperf. of Dujir (to be
               bored, to be restless), conjugated like
               Tuli9 in Chapter VI.

bil9aks: on the contrary, the opposite.

Hafleet: parties, festivities, Hafle (sing.).

sahraat: evening parties, evening performances, sahra (sing.).

needi: club, association, naweedi (pl.).

yil9abu: they play. Imperf. of li9ib (to play, to perform), conjugated like ∫irib in Chapter II.

jiraan: neighbors, jaar (sing.).

'raayibun: their relatives.

yitGayyar: it changes. Imperf. of tGayyar (to undergo changes, to be modified), conjugated like t'axxar in Chapter XII.

tsa"i9:   it becomes cold. Imperf. of sa"a9 (to become cold), conjugated like 9arraf in Chapter II.

dini: nature, earth, world.

ma bit9uud: will no longer be. Expression made of the negative particle ma and the Imperf. of verb 9aad (to return, to come back), conjugated like keen in Chapter II.

∫arrfuuna: honor us with your visit, come on over. Imp. of ∫arraf (to honor), conjugated like 9arraf in Chapter II.

Grammar Notes

• **zaar (to visit)** is a Measure I Hollow verb.

Pronoun	Perfect	Imperfect	Imperative
huwwe	zaar	yzuur	
hiyyi	zaarit	tzuur	
hinni	zaaru	yzuuru	
inta	zurt	tzuur	zuur
inti	zurti	tzuuri	zuuri
intu	zurtu	tzuuru	zuuru
ana	zurt	zuur	
niHna	zurna	nzuur	

• **'arrar (to decide)** is a Measure II verb.

Pronoun	Perfect	Imperfect	Imperative
huwwe	'arrar	y'arrir	
hiyyi	'arrarit	t'arrir	
hinni	'arraru	y'arriru	
inta	'arrart	t'arrir	'arrir
inti	'arrarti	t'arriri	'arriri
intu	'arrartu	t'arriru	'arriru
ana	'arrart	'arrir	
niHna	'arrarna	n'arrir	

Other Useful Vocabulary

Elements (maweed)

fire	naar
soil, earth	traab, arD
water	may
wind	hawa

Nature (Tabii9a)

beach	ʃaT, plaaj
creek	see'ye
flower	zahra, zhuur (pl.).
grass	Haʃiiʃ
lake	buHayra
mud	waHl
plain	sahl
river	nahr, anhur (pl.).
sand	raml
sea	baHr
sky	sama, jaw
tree	sajra, sajar (pl.).
valley	waadi, widyeen (pl.).
waves	mawj

Weather

cloud	Gaym
cold	bard
frost	jliid
hail	barad
hot, warm	ʃawb
lightning	bar'
storm	9aaSfe
thunder	ra9d

Adjectives describing the sea

| calm | reeyi', heede |

clean	nDiif
dangerous	xuTir
dirty	wusix, mwassax
polluted	mlawwas
wavy	heeyij

REINFORCEMENT

• Describe the weather today.

• Describe the climate where you live.

• What is your favorite season? Why?

• Where would you like to spend your summer vacation? Why?

• Do you prefer the mountains or the beach? Why?

Chapter Fifteen
Courtesy Expressions & Interjections

In this chapter you will learn about appropriate expressions and interjections for a variety of occasions.

Happy Occasions (afraaH)

Engagement (xuTbe)

- mabruuk   congratulations
- xuTbe mbaarake   may your engagement be blessed

Wedding (zaweej, 9urs)

- mabruuk ya 9ariis   congratulations groom
- mabruuk ya 9aruus   congratulations bride
- nʃalla btithannu   wishing you happiness
- kil iyyeemkun afraaH   may all your days be happy
- 9a'beelak, 9a'beelik.... may your turn come

Birth (wileede)

- mabruuk-TTufl   congratulations on the baby
- *alla y9ayyʃu   may God give him a long life
- nʃalla byislam   may God keep him safe

Baptism, Christening (9meede)

- 9meede mbaarke   may this baptism be blessed
- nʃalla bit9ammdu-l'ixwe may you baptize the siblings

Return from pilgrimage to Mecca (Hajj)

- Hajj mabruur wsa9y maʃkuur
  may your pilgrimage be blessed and
  your ritual walk be praiseworthy

Success in business, career, or exam (najeeH)

- mabruuk   congratulations
- tahaniina   our best wishes
- *alla ywaffi'   may God grant you success

Holidays (a9yeed)

- kil 9iid w'inta bxayr   may every holiday you be
                               in good health
- 9iid mbaarak   happy (blessed) holiday

SAD OCCASIONS (aHzeen)

Accidents, tragedies (Haweedis, kaweeris)

- lHamdilla 9assaleeme   thank God for your safety
- *alla ySabbirkun   may God give you patience
- *alla y'awwikun   may God give you strength
- mniiH-lmiʃ a9Zam   lucky it was not worse

Sickness (maraD)

- saleemtak   wishing you feel better
- *alla yiʃfiik   may God give you speedy
                             recovery
- *alla y'addimlak-   may God improve your
  SSuHHa   health

Death (mawt)

- *alla yirHamu   God have mercy on him
- l9awaD bisaleemtak   may you be compensated by your well-being
- inna lillaah   we belong to God
- ta9aazina   our condolences

OTHER SOCIAL OCCASIONS (munesabeet ijtimee9iyye)

Going on a trip (safar)

- *alla ykuun ma9ak   may God be with you
- nʃalla tuSal bissaleeme   may you arrive safely
- safra mwaff'a   have a successful trip
- truuH wtirja9   may you go and
  bissaleeme   return safely

Return from a trip (rjuu9 min-ssafar)

- lHamdilla 9awSuulak bissaleeme
  thank God for your safe arrival

Moving to a new home (na'liyye)

- na'liyye mbaarke   hope the move is a blessed one
- mabruuk-lbayt   congratulations on the house

Coming out of the shower (duuʃ) or the barbershop (Hillee')

- na9iiman   hope you enjoyed it

At the table (9al'akl)

- Sahtayn   enjoy your food, bon appétit

- keesak   cheers, to your health
- sufra deeyme   may your table be always
                      bountiful (at the end of the meal)

If someone sneezes (9aTas)

- SuHHa   health
- naʃu   elation

If someone is wearing new clothes, or acquiring something new.

- mabruuk (lfustaan, ljizdeen, etc...)   congratulations

INTERJECTIONS

aH	reacting to something cold or hot
aax	expressing pain
bas	enough
nya9'	expressing disgust
oof	sigh of boredom or annoyance
tfeh	disgust or anger (similar to spitting)
Tuz	big deal, see if I care
yalla	come on, move it, hurry up
yaay	excitement, admiration
xay	sigh of relief, or smelling good aroma
9ayb	shame, disgrace

BODY LANGUAGE

Raising eyebrows, head or shoulders is a negative answer. This may be accompanied by the sound /tse/, produced by the tongue rubbing roughly backward on the upper teeth and the palate.

Nodding head and raising eyebrows is a sign of admiration. This may be accompanied by the sound /biʃ/.

APPENDIX

In this appendix you will find an extended list of the vocabulary related to all the topics presented in this book. This may help those who do not have the time to learn all the components included in it, and those who only need certain words to survive on a short trip. **It is important however to study the phonetic system in the beginning of the book in order to pronounce the vocabulary correctly.** This Appendix can be an excellent addendum to any travel guide book on Lebanon.

Chapter One: Greetings & Formalities

FORMAL GREETINGS

In the morning: SabaaH-lxayr   "Good morning"
In the evening: masa-lxayr   "Good evening"

OTHER FORMS OF GREETING

assalaamu 9alaykum   "Peace be upon you"
marHaba   "Hi, Hello"
In the evening: sa9iide   "pleasant evening"
In a working environment:
9aweefe or ya9tiik-l9aafye "wishing you health"

If you are addressing someone in particular you may use the vocative (ya) before his/her name, e.g. marHaba ya *samiir.

In the following exchanges you will become familiar with some Lebanese names, and you will learn how to greet people and answer their greetings.

*sa9iid: SabaaH-lxayr ya *9aaTif
*9aaTif: ahlan, SabaaH-nnuur ya *sa9iid

*9afaaf: masa-lxayr ya *Hanaan
*Hanaan: masa-nnuur ya *9afaaf

*Hasan: assalamu 9alaykum ya *9adnaan
*9adnaan: wa9alaykumu-ssalaam ya *Hasan

*xaaled: marHaba ya *hiʃaam
*hiʃaam: marHabtayn ya *xaaled

*sihaam: 9aweefe ya *huda
*huda: alla y9afiiki ya *sihaam

*9umar: sa9iide ya *Haliim
*Haliim: yis9ud ha-lmasa ya *9umar

Greetings are usually followed by common courtesy questions, e.g. (kifak) How are you? (kiif-lHaal) How is it going? etc... . Middle Easterns always thank (*alla) God for their well being.

*samiir: marhaba ya *salwa
*salwa: ahlan *samiir, kiifak?
*samiir: lHamdilla, kiifik inti?
*salwa: nuʃkur *alla meeʃe-lHaal

(ahlan) is an expression used to welcome someone, or to answer someone's greeting. It means literally: you are among your family.

(kiif) is an interrogative meaning "how". Verb "to be" is implied in pronouns or pronominal suffixes like ik. ak, etc... (kiifak) means: how are you, masculine, singular .

(inti) is a feminine singular pronoun.

Please note that in the leb. dialect the fem. pl. pron. and pronominal suffixes are replaced by the masc. pl. pron. and pronominal suffixes. The dual pron. are replaced by the masc. pl. pronouns. **In all examples of the explanatory notes, I used the masc. sing. form.**

PRONOUNS

he, him	huwwe
she, her	hiyyi
they, them	hinni
you (masc. sing.)	inta
you (fem. sing.)	inti
you (masc. & fem. pl.)	intu
I, me	ana
we, us	niHna

PRONOMINAL SUFFIXES

When pronominal suffixes are added to a noun they indicate possession, e.g. baytak (your home, masc. sing.), ismak (your name, masc. sing.); when added to a verb they are considered direct or indirect objects of that verb. e.g. ʃeefak (he saw you).

u	masc. sing. (his)	baytu	ismu
a	fem. sing.(her)	bayta	isma
un	masc. & fem. pl.(your)	baytun	ismun
ak	masc. sing. (your)	baytak	ismak
ik	fem. sing. (your)	baytik	ismik
kun	masc. & fem. pl. (your)	baytkun	ismkun
i	(my)	bayti	ismi
na	(our)	baytna	ismna

Some Useful Interrogatives

how	kiif
how much	'iddayʃ
how many	kam waaHad
what	ʃu
who	miin
where	wayn
when	aymta
which	ayya
why	layʃ
what does it mean	ʃu ya9ni
what is your name	ʃu ismak (masc. sing)
what is this	ʃu hayda

Other Useful Vocabulary

yes	na9am
no	la'
if possible	iza mumkin
if you please	9muul ma9ruuf
perhaps	bijuuz
correct, true	SaHiiH
of course	Tab9an
wrong, incorrect	GalaT
thank you	ʃukran
a reply to ʃukran	9afwan (do not mention it, you are welcome)
my name is	ismi
I want	baddi
here	hawne
give me	9Tiini
a little	ʃway, nitfe
a lot	ktiir
later	ba9deen

NATIONALITIES

American	amerkeeni
Australian	ustraali
British	ingliizi
Canadian	kanadi
French	frinseewi
German	ulmaani
Lebanese	libneeni
Polish	poloni
Russian	ruusi
Spanish	spanyoli

Chapter Two: Socializing & Family Members

DEMONSTRATIVES

this, masc. sing.	hayda, e.g. hayda *saliim (this is *saliim)
this, fem. sing.	haydi, e.g. haydi *samia (this is *samia)
these, masc. & fem. pl.	hawdi, e.g. hawdi *samia w*saliim (these are *samia and *saliim)
those, masc. & fem. pl.	hawdiik,e.g. hawdiik *samia w*saliim

CONJUNCTION

and	/w/ e.g. *saliim w*saami (*saliim and *saami)

SOCIALIZING

welcome	ahla wsahla
come on in	tfaDDal

nice to meet you	tʃarrafna
good bye	bxaatrak
reply to good bye	ma9-ssaleeme (go with peace)
happy	mabsuuT
cup of coffee	finjeen 'ahwe
cup of tea	finjeen ʃaay
let's go	yalla
hurry up	yalla yalla, 9ajjil

FAMILY MEMBERS & RELATIVES

father	bayy, bayyeet (pl.)
mother	imm, immeet (pl.)
brother	xayy, ixwe (pl.)
sister	uxt, xayyeet (pl.)
son	ibn, wleed (pl.)
daughter	bint, baneet (pl.)
grand father	jid, jduud (pl.)
grand mother	sit, sitteet (pl.)
uncle	9amm (paternal side) , 9muum (pl.)
	xeel, (maternal side) xweel (pl.)
aunt	9ammi (paternal side), 9ammeet (pl.)
	xeele (maternal side), xeleet (pl.)
cousin (masc.)	ibn 9amm or ibn xaal
cousin (fem.)	bint 9amm or bint xaal
brother-in-law	Suhr, Shuuraat (pl.)
mother-in-law	Hama, Hamaweet (pl.)
daughter-in-law	kinni, kneeyin (pl.)
parents	ahl

OTHER USEFUL VOCABULARY

lady, Mrs.	madaam
Miss	madmuzeel
sir, mister	xaweeja

Chapter Three: Dates & Numbers

CARDINAL NUMBERS

one	waaHad (does not modify nouns, it only follows a noun for emphasis).
two	tnayn (does not modify nouns, use dual form instead as seen before).
three	tleete
four	arb9a
five	xamse
six	sitte
seven	sab9a
eight	tmeene
nine	tis9a
ten	9aʃra
eleven	Hda9ʃ
twelve	tna9ʃ
thirteen	tletta9ʃ
fourteen	arba9ta9ʃ
fifteen	xamsta9ʃ
sixteen	sitta9ʃ
seventeen	saba9ta9ʃ
eighteen	tmenta9ʃ
nineteen	tisa9ta9ʃ
twenty	9iʃriin
twenty one	waaHad w9iʃriin
twenty two	tnayn w9iʃriin...
thirty	tletiin
thirty one	waaHad witletiin...
forty	arb9iin
fifty	xamsiin
sixty	sittiin
seventy	sab9iin
eighty	tmeniin
ninety	tis9iin

Numbers from 3-10 are followed by the plural form of the noun they modify. They also lose their final vowel before than noun, e.g. xams byuut, 9aʃr se9aat

Numbers from 11 on are followed by the singular form of the noun they modify, e.g. 9iʃriin bayt.

Numbers from 11-19 take /ar/ before the noun they modify, e.g. xamsta9ʃar bayt.

hundred	miyyi
hundred one	miyyi wwaaHad
hundred two...	miyyi witnayn
two hundred	mitayn
three hundred	tleet miyyi
thousand	alf
million	malyuun
billion	milyaar

ORDINAL NUMBERS

first	awwal (masc.), uula (fem.)
second	teeni / teenye
third	teelit / teelte
fourth	raabi9 / raab9a
fifth	xeemis / xeemse
sixth	seedis / seedse
seventh	seebi9 / seeb9a
eighth	teemin / teemne
nineth	teesi9 / tees9a
tenth	9eeʃir / 9eeʃra
last	eexir

Ordinal numbers after tenth are not communly used, they are replaced by the word "ra'm" which means number followed by a cardinal number after the singular form of the noun, e.g. "bayt ra'm Hda9ʃ", house number eleven, instead of the eleventh house.

FRACTIONS AND EXPRESSIONS RELATED TO NUMBERS

quarter	rib9
third	tilt
half	nuSS
a little	ʃway, nitfe
a lot	ktiir
minus	illa

Days of the week (ayyaam l'usbuu9)

day   yawm, nhaar
week   jim9a, usbuu9

Sunday	l'aHad	Thursday	lxamiis
Monday	ttanayn	Friday	ljim9a
Tuesday	ttaleeta	Saturday	ssabet
Wednesday	l'urb9a		

Months of the year (aʃhur-ssini)

month   ʃahr
year   sini

January	kaanuun-tteeni
February	ʃbaaT
March	azaar
April	niseen
May	ayyaar
June	Hzayraan
July	tammuuz
August	aab
September	ayluul
October	tiʃriinl'awwal
November	tiʃriin-tteeni
December	kaanuun-l'awwal

The Seasons (alfuSuul)

Season	faSl
Winter	ʃʃiti
Spring	rrabii9
Summer	SSayf
Fall	lxariif

EXPRESSIONS RELATED TO TIME

moment	laHZa
second	takki
minute	d'ii'a
now	halla'
later	ba9deen
today	lyawm
tomorrow	bukra
yesterday	mbeeriH
evening	9aʃiyyi, lmasa
night	layl
morning	SubH
noon	Duhr
week-end	wiikend

OTHER USEFUL VOCABULARY

welcome back	lHamdilla 9a-ssaleeme
trip	safra, raHle
long	Tawiil
almost	ta'riiban
aircraft	Tiyyaara
school	madrasi, madeeris (pl.)
because	li'annu
great	9aZiim
here	hawn
class, course	Saff, Sfuuf (pl.)
around, about	Haweele, ʃi
almost	ta'riiban
after	ba9d
before	'abl
it is a must	leezim

Chapter Four: Telephone & Post Office

AT THE POST OFFICE (markaz-lbariid)

address	9inwaan
airmail	jawwi
certified	msawgar, maDmuun
employee	mwaZZaf, mwaZfiin (pl.)
envelope	mGallaf, mGallfeet (pl.); Zarf, Zruufe (pl.)
heavy	t'iil
important	mhimm
in order to	Hatta
it depends	Hasab
letter	maktuub, mketiib (pl.)
light	xafiif
mail	bariid
mailbox	Sanduu'-lbariid
package	pakee, 9ilbe, Tard
postcard	kart postaal
scale	mizeen
sender	mursil
stamps	Tawaabi9, wara' buul
value	'iime
weigh	wazn
window	ʃibbeek

ON THE PHONE

available	mawjuud
answering machine	msajjle, répondeur
at any rate	9ala kil Haal
busy	maʃGuul
international	duwali
line	xaTT
may be	mumkin, bijuuz
message	xabar
operator	santralist

phone call	muxaabara
public phone	heetif 9muumi
static	tiʃwiiʃ
telephone book	daliil-lhaatif
to dial	Talab-rra'm
to hang up	sakkar-lxaTT, Tabaʃ-ssemmee9a
to pick up receiver	rafa9-ssemmee9a
until	Hatta
voice	Sawt

Chapter Five: Biographical Information & Means of Transportation

BIOGRAPHY

age	9umr
black	aswad, sawda (fem.)
blond	aʃ'ar, ʃa'ra (fem.)
brown	asmar, samra (fem.) olive skin
building	bineeye
divorced	mTalla', mTall'a (fem.)
educated	mit9allim
employee	mwaZZaf
height	Tuul
identity	hawiyye
married	mjawwaz, mjawwze (fem.)
photo	Suura
profession	mihni
short	'aSiir, 'aSiire (fem.)
single	a9zab, 9azbe (fem.)
student	Taalib
tall	Tawiil, Tawiile (fem.)
weight	wazn
white	abyaD, bayDa (fem.)
work	ʃuGl, waZiife

Christian	masiiHi
Druze	dirzi
Jewish	yehuudi
Maronite	maruuni
Moslem	mislim
Shiite	ʃii9i
Sunni	sinni

MEANS OF TRANSPORTATION

air, space	jaww, faDa
bicycle	bisikleet
land	arD, barr
road	Tarii'
sea	baHr
travel	safar
aircraft	Tiyyara
airport	maTaar
boat	markab, babor, beexra
bus	otobuus
driver	ʃofœr
fast	sarii9
line, route	xaT, xTuuT (pl.)
motorcycle	motosikl
parking	parkin, maw'af
passenger	reekib, rikkeeb (pl.)
port	por, marfa'
porter	9itteel, 9ittele (pl.)
road light	iʃaara, iʃaraat (pl.)
rocket	Saruux
seat	ma'9ad, ma'ee9id (pl.)
slow	baTii'
small boat	ʃaxtura
taxi	taksi
ticket	tiket, biTaa'a, tazkara
tire	duleeb, dweliib (pl.)

to declare	SarraH
to drive	saa', ysuu' (imperf.)
to beep	zammar (to beep the horn)
to brake	Darab freem
to pass	'aTa9, dawbal (it also means to repeat an academic year).
to reserve	Hajaz
to stop	wa"af
to wait	naTar
train	treen

OTHER USEFUL VOCABULARY

arrival	wuSuul
arrow	sihm, fleeʃ
bathroom	Himmeem
claim	'asiime
customs	jamaarik
delay	ti'xiir
door	beeb, bweeb (pl.)
emergency	Tawaari'
empty	faaDi
foreigner	ajnabi
full	mitleen
hitch-hiking	otostop
key	mifteeH
map	xaarTa
passport	paspor, jawaaz safar
price	si9r
prohibited	mamnuu9
seat	ma'9ad
smoking	tidxiin
suitcase	ʃanTa
visa	viza, ta'ʃiirit duxuul
wind	hawa
window	ʃibbeek, ʃbebiik (pl.)

Chapter Six: Directions & Road Conditions

Colors. Adjectives of color follow the noun they modify.

	Masc.	**Fem.**	**Pl.**
beige	beej		
black	aswad	sawda	suud
blue	azra'	zar'a	zir'
brown	binni	binniyyi	
gold	dihabi		
green	axDar	xaDra	xuDr
gray	rmeedi	rmeediyyi	
navy blue	kiHli	kiHliyyi	
orange	bird'aani		
pink	zahr		
red	aHmar	Hamra	Humr
silver	fuDDi		
violet	banafsaji		
white	abyaD	bayDa	biiD
yellow	aSfar	Safra	Sufr

Directions

above	faw'
after	ba9d
behind	wara, xalf
before	'abl
close	'ariib
down	taHt
far	b9iid
here	hawn
in front	iddeem
inside	juwwa, inside something: bi'alb, e.g. bi'alb-lbayt: inside the house
near	Hadd, janb

on	9ala
outside	barra
there	huniik
up	faw'

ROAD CONDITIONS

clean	nDiif, nDiife (fem.)
check point	Heejiz
dangerous	xuTra
dirty	mijwi, mijwiyye (fem.)
empty	faaDe, faaDye (fem.)
hole	juura, juwar (pl.)
icy	mjallad, mjallde (fem.)
litter	zbeele
middle	nuSS
narrow	Dayyi', Dayy'a (fem.)
paved	mzaffat, mzaffatte (fem.)
safe	eemne
side	Taraf
slippery	bitzaHHit
ticket	ZabT
wide	9ariiD, 9ariiDa (fem.); weesi9, wees9a (fem.)

OTHER USEFUL VOCABULARY

behind	wara
big	kbiir
building	bineeye, bineyeet (pl.)
center	markaz, maraakiz (pl.)
end	eexir
excuse me	bil'zn
exit	mafra', mafeeri' (pl.)
far	b9iid
first of all	awwal ʃi

flag	9alam
floor	Taabi', Twaabi' (pl.)
fortress	'al9a, 'lee9 (pl.)
highway	otostraad
near	'ariib
next to	Hadd
never	abadan
municipality	baladiyye
public square	seeHa, seHaat (pl.)
road	Tarii', Turu' (pl.)
sign	aarma, armaat (pl.)
small	zGiir
to the left	9aʃʃmeel
to the right	9alyemiin
towards	Sawb
traffic jam	9aj'it sayr
when	lamma (not interrogative)

Chapter Seven: Food & Nutrition

Food (akl)

Vegetables (xuDra)

artichoke	arDiʃʃawke
asparagus	halyuun
beens (green)	luubye xaDra
(kidney)	faSulya
(lima)	faSulya 9ariiDa
beet	ʃmandar
cabbage	malfuuf
carrot	jazar
cauliflower	arnabiiT
corn	dara
cucumber	xyaar
eggplant	batinjeen

leeks	sil'
lentils	9adas
lettuce	xass
onion	baSal
potato	baTaTa
rice	ruzz
spinach	sbeenix
squash	kuusa
tomato	banaduura

Meats (laHm)

beef	ba'ar
chicken	djeej
duck	baTT
fish	samak
frog	Dafaadi9
lamb	Ganam
veal	9ijl

Fruits (fweeke)

almond	lawz
apple	tiffeeH
apricot	miʃmuʃ
banana	mawz
cherry	karaz
fig	tiin
grape	9inab
lemon	laymuun HaamuD
melon	ʃimmeem
olive	zaytuun
orange	laymuun
peach	dirraa'
pear	njaaS

plum	xawx
tangerine	afandi
watermelon	baTTiiX

Spices (bharaat)

garlic	tuum
mint	na9na9
mustard	xardal
parsley	ba'duunis
pepper	bhaar
salt	milH
sesame	simsum

AT THE RESTAURANT (bil-maT9am)

ashtray	manfDa
bread	xibz
chair	kirse
cup	finjeen
dish	SaHn
fork	ʃawke
glass	kibbeeye
knife	sikkiin
napkin	fuuTa
oil	zayt
saltshaker	mamlaHa
spoon	mal9'a
table	Taawle
tableclothe	ʃarʃaf
vinegar	xall

BEVERAGES (maʃrubeet)

| beer | biira |
| juice | 9aSiir |

lemonade	laymunaaDa
milk	Haliib
water	mayy
wine	nbiid

PERSONAL REACTIONS

disgusted	'irfeen
full	ʃib9aan
hungry	juu9aan
starving	mxawwar
thirsty	9aTʃaan

OTHER FOOD RELATED VOCABULARY

baked	bilfurn
boiled	masluu'
breast	Sudr
butter	zibde
cake	gato
cheese	jibne
eggs	bayD
flour	THiin
fried	mi'le
grilled	miʃwe
leg	faxd
liver	'aSbe
peanuts	fistu'
pickles	kabiis
wings	jweeniH
yeast	xamiire
yogurt	laban

OTHER USEFUL VOCABULARY

apetizers	mezeet

big plate	jaaT, juuT (pl.)
bottle	'anniini
breakfast	tirwii'a
busy	maʃGuul
chopping	farm
cold	beerid
dinner	9aʃa
dish	SaHn, SHuun (pl.)
fresh	Taaza
great	9aZiim
hot	suxn
if possible	iza mumkin
instead	badl, maTraH
invitation	9aziime
items, things	iʃya
never mind	basiiTa
ready	HaaDir
salad	salaTa
table	Taawle
time	wa't
waiter	garson, meetr

Chapter Eight: Clothing

MAN'S CLOTHING (malbuseet rijjeliyye)

bathing suit	mayo
belt	'ʃaaT
boots	bot
bowtie	papiyon
briefs	sliip
gloves	kfuuf
handkerchief	maHrame, mHeerim (pl.)
hat	burnaytTa
jacket	jakeet, jaketeet (pl.)
jeans	jiinz
necktie	kravaat

pajamas	pijaama
pants	pantalon
raincoat	tranʃkot
sandals	Sundaal, Snadiil (pl.)
sneekers	spadri
suit	Ta'm, T'uume (pl.)
suspenders	bruteleet
T-shirt	tiʃœrt
undershirt	fanella
tuxedo	smokin
vest	Sudriyye
wallet	maHfZa

WOMAN'S CLOTHING (malbuseet nisweniyye)

blouse	bluuze
bra	Sudriyye, Sdaari (pl.)
change purse	jizdeen zGiir
coat	kabbuut, kbebiit (pl.)
dress	fusTaan, fsaTiin (pl.)
evening gown	fustaan tawiil, fustaan sahra
fur coat	kabbuut faru
high heel	ka9b 9aali
pantyhose	kollan
scarf	iʃarp
shoes	skarbiine
skirt	tannuura, tneniir (pl.)
slip full	kombinezon
socks	kalseet
suit	tayyœr
underwear	kilot

FABRICS ('meeʃ)

cashmere	kaʃmiir
cotton	'uTun
flannel	fanella

gabardine	gavardiin
leather	jild
nylon	naylon
polyester	polyester
silk	Hariir
wool	Suuf

SIZES ('yeseet)

big	kbiir
long	Tawiil
medium	wasaT
short	'aSiir
small	zGiir
tight	Dayyi'
wide	weesi9, 9ariiD

OTHER USEFUL VOCABULARY

appointment	maw9ad
closet	xzeene, xzeneet (pl.)
confused	meHtaar, meHtaara (fem.)
ear rings	Hala'
formal	rasmi
full	mitleen, mitleene (fem.)
hairdresser	Hillaa'
idea	fikra, afkaar (pl.)
neckless	9a'd, 9'uude (pl.)
pair	jawz
party	Hafle, Hafleet
perhaps	barki,
pretty	Helu, Hilwe (fem.)
purse	jizdeen
sleeve	kim
suitable	xarj
sweater	kanze

Chapter Nine: Health & Medical Problems

THE HUMAN BODY (jism-l'inseen)

	Sing.	Pl.(most common)
ankle	keeHil	kweeHil
back	Dahr	
bladder	mabwale	
blood	damm	
body	jism	ajseem
bone	9aDme	9Daam
brain	nxaa9	nxa9aat
breast	Sudr	Sduura
cheek	xadd	xduud
chest	Sudr	
chin	da'n	d'uun
ear	dayne	dinayn
elbow	kuu9	kwee9
eye	9ayn	9yuun
face	wijj	wjeeh
finger	uSbi9	'Sabii9
foot	ijr	
gum	niire	
hand	iid	ayeede
head	raas	ruus
heart	'alb	'luub
hip	wirk	wraak
jaw	fak	
joint	mafSal	mafaSil
kidney	kilwe	kleewe
knee	rikbe	rikab
leg	faxd	fxaad
lip	ʃiffe	ʃfeef
liver	kibid	kbeed
lung	riyya	raweeya

mouth	timm	tmeem
muscle	9aDal	9aDalaat
nail	Dufr	Dafiir
neck	ra'be	r'eeb
nerve	9aSab	a9Saab
nose	munxaar	mnexiir
shoulder	kitf	kteef
skin	jild	jluud
stomach	baTn, mi9di	
throat	zla9iim, Hunjra	Haneejir
vein	9ir', ʃiryeen	9ruu', ʃrayiin

Commom Illnesses

blood pressure	DaGt (9aali: high; waaTi: low)
cold	raʃH
constipation	imseek, kteem
cough	sa9le
diarrhea	sheel
dizziness	dawxa
infection	iltiheeb
inflammation	waram
insomnia	'ala'
heartburn	Har'a
hemorrhage	naziif

Some Serious Illnesses

AIDS	sida
cancer	saraTaan
diabetes	sikkari
heart attack	kriza bil'alb
jaundice	Sfayra
paralysis	ʃalal
tuberculosis	sill

ulcer   'irHa

SOME HANDICAPS

	Masc.	Fem.	Pl.
blind	a9ma	9amya	9imyeen
cross-eyed	aHwal	Hawla	Huul
crazy	axwat,	xawta,	xuut,
	majnuun	majnuune	mjeniin
deaf	aTraʃ	Tarʃa	Turʃ
lame	a9raj	9arja	9irj
mute	axras	xarsa	xirs
paralyzed	maʃluul	maʃluule	maʃluliin

SOME INJURIES

fracture   kisr
ligament sprain   falʃit 9ruu'
sprain   fikʃ

VACCINES (Tu9m)

measles   HaSbi
mumps   buk9ayb
polio   ʃalal
smallpox   jidri

OTHER USEFUL VOCABULARY

accident   Haadis, Haweedis (pl.)
ambulance   is9aaf
body   jism, badan
fever   Haraara
feverish   maHruur
hospital   mistaʃfa

it looks   mbayyan
medication   dawa, idwye (pl.)
pain   waja9, awjee9 (pl.)
physician   Hakiim, doktœr
sick   saaxin, mariiD

Chapter Ten: Professions & Careers

SKILLED WORKERS

baker   furraan
barber   Hillee'
blacksmith   Hiddeed
butcher   laHHaam
carpenter   nijjaar
electrician   kihrabji
plumber   sangari
shoe repair   kindarji
taylor   xiyyaaT
tile layer   bullaaT

OTHER PROFESSIONALS (miHtirfiin)

engineer   mhandis
journalist   SaHaafi
lawyer   muHaami
nurse   mmarriD
officer   ZaabiT
professor   profesœr
physician   doktœr, Hakiim
pilot   Tiyyarji

ARTISTS (finneniin)

artist   finneen

musician	musi'aar
painter	risseem
photographer	mSawwir
poet	ʃee9ir, ʃu9ara (pl.)
sculptor	niHHaat
singer	mGanni, muTrib
writer	keetib

Politicians (siyasiyyi)

ambassador	safiir, sufara (pl.)
consul	'unSul, 'anaaSil (pl.)
deputy	neeyib, nuwweeb (pl.)
governor	Heekim, muHaafiZ
judge	'aaDi
mayor	muxtaar
minister	waziir, wuzara (pl.)
president	ra'iis

Other Useful Vocabulary

accounting	muHeesabi
building site	warʃe, wiraʃ (pl.)
college	killiyyi
company	ʃirke, ʃirkeet (pl.)
engineering	handasi
family	9ayle, 9iyal (pl.)
high school	sanawiyye
insurance	Damaan
law	H'uu'
medicine	Tubb
meeting	ijtimee9
school	madrasi, madeeris (pl.)
university	jeem9a, jeem9aat (pl.)
work	ʃuGl

Chapter Eleven: Housing & Living Conditions

THE HOUSE (al-bayt)

balcony	balkon
bathroom	Himmeem
bell	jaras
ceiling	sa'f
concrete	baTon
dining room	'uDit-ssufra
door	beeb, bweeb (pl.)
floor	arD
garden	jnayne
inside	juwwa
key	mifteeH, mfetiiH (pl.)
kitchen	maTbax
living room	daar
madxal	entrance
outside	barra
roof	saTH
room	'uuDa, 'uwaD (pl.)
stone	Hajar
window	ʃibbeek, ʃbebiik (pl.)
wood	xaʃab

APPLIANCES

dishwasher	jilleeye
dryer	niʃʃeefe
freezer	tilleeje
juicer	9iSSaara
microwave	mikro'ond
refrigerator	birraad
stove	furn
television	televizyon

washer   Gisseele

FURNITURE (farʃ, 9afʃ) and others

bed   taxt, txuuti (pl.)
chair   kirsi, karaasi (pl.)
couch   Sofa
cup   finjeen, fnejiin (pl.)
fork   ʃawke, ʃuwak (pl.)
glass   kibbeeye
knife   sikkiin, skekiin (pl.)
spoon   mal9'a
table   Taawle

BEDDING

blanket   Hreem
comforter   lHeef
matress   farʃe, firaʃ (pl.)
pillow   mxadde
sheet   ʃarʃaf, ʃaraaʃif (pl.)

THE BATHROOM

bathtub   maGTas
bidet   bide
faucet   Hanafiyye
toilet   twaleet
toilet paper   wara' twaleet
toilet tank   sifon
towel   manʃafe
sink   maGsale

CLEANING TOOLS

broom   miknse

brush	firʃeeye
bucket	dalu
mop	mamsHa
shovel	majruud
sponge	sfinje

OTHER USEFUL VOCABULARY

always	deeyman
apartment	ʃi"a, ʃi'a' (pl.)
electricity	kahraba
elevator	asonsœr
entrance	madxal
expenses	mSariif
furniture	farʃ, 9afʃ
guest	Dayf, Dyuuf (pl.)
hair dryer	seʃwaar
heating	ʃofaaj
janitor	naTuur, nwaTiir (pl.)
maid	Saan9a, Sunnee9 (pl.)
maintenance	Siyaani
neighborhood	Hayy, iHya (pl.)
new	jdiid
old	'adiim
out of order	miʃ meeʃi
owner	SaaHib-lmilk
parking	garaaj
rent	ajaar
shelf	raff
stairs	daraj
tenant	mista'jir
wall	HayT, HiTaan (pl.)

Chapter Twelve: Hobbies & Leisure Activities

SPORTS (riyaaDa)

basketball	basketbol, kurat-ssalla
boxing	muleekame, boks
game	matʃ, mubaraat
golf	golf
judo	judo
karate	karate
ping pong	pinpon, kurat-TTaawle
skiing	ski
soccer	futbol, kurat-lQadam
swimming	sbeeHa
tennis	tenis, kurat-lmaDrib
volleyball	volibol, kurat-TTaa'ira
water ski	skinotiik, tazalluj 9almay
wrestling	muSaara9a
to be even	t9eedal
to lose	xisir
to win	ribiH

HOBBIES (hiwayeet) & LEISURE ACTIVITIES (tasliye)

acting	timsiil
correspondence	mureesale
dancing	ra'S
diving	GaTs
drawing	tuSwiir, rasm
fishing	Sayd-ssamak
horseback riding	rikb-lxayl
hunting	Sayd
running	rakD
sculpting	naHt
singing	Gina
stamp collecting	jam9 Tawaabi9
swimming	sbeeHa
travelling	safar

MUSICAL INSTRUMENTS

accordion	akkordeyon
flute	naay
guitar	gitaar
organ	org
piano	pyano
violin	vyolon, kamanja

OTHER USEFUL VOCABULARY

exhibition	ma9raD, ma9aariD (pl.)
famous	maʃhuur
game	matʃ
hotel	oteel
movie	film
place	maTraH, maTaariH (pl.)
playing	li9b
seat	ma'9ad, ma'ee9id (pl.)
similar	mitl
stadium, field	mal9ab, malee9ib (pl.)
stress	HaSr
team	farii', fira' (pl.)
theater play	masraHiyye
voice	Sawt

Chapter Thirteen: Mishaps & Offenses

CRIMES AND MISDEMEANORS (jaraayim, muxelafeet)

beating	Darb
fighting	maʃkal, 9arke
kidnapping	xaTf
lying	kizb
murder	'atl, jariime
rape	iGtiSaab

theft	sir'a
threat	tihdiid
vandalism	tixriib

CRIMINALS (mujrimiin)

crook	az9ar
criminal	mujrim
gang	9iSaabe
thief	sirree', Haraami

JUSTICE (9adl)

court	maHkame
judge	'aaDi
lawyer	muHaami
witness	ʃeehid

ACCIDENTS (Haweedis)

damage	xaraab
drowning	Gara'
earthquake	hazze, zilzeel
flood	fayaDaan

OTHER USEFUL VOCABULARY

afraid	xeeyif, fiz9aan
crime	jariime, jaraayim (pl.)
distance	maseefe
expert	xabiir, xubara (pl.)
fire	Harii'a, naar
high	9eele
human	inseen
information	ma9lumeet
injured	jariiH, jirHa (pl.)

ladder	sillum, sleelim (pl.)
low	waaTe
people	nees, 9aalam
report	ti'riir, ta'ariir (pl.)
safety	amn
situation	Heele
smoke	daxne, dixxaan
war	Harb

Chapter Fourteen: Nature & Climate

ELEMENTS (maweed)

fire	naar
soil, earth	traab, arD
water	mayy
wind	hawa

NATURE (Tabii9a)

beach	ʃaT, plaaj
creek	see'ye
flower	zahra, zhuur (pl.).
grass	Haʃiiʃ
lake	buHayra
mud	waHl
plain	sahl
river	nahr, anhur (pl.).
sand	raml
sea	baHr
sky	sama, jaww
tree	sajra, sajar (pl.).
valley	waadi
waves	mawj

WEATHER

cloud	Gaym
cold	bard
frost	jliid
hail	barad
hot, warm	ʃawb
lightning	bar'
storm	9aaSfe
thunder	ra9d

ADJECTIVES DESCRIBING THE SEA

calm	reeyi', heede
clean	nDiif
dangerous	xuTir
dirty	wusix, mwassax
polluted	mlawwas
wavy	heeyij

OTHER USEFUL VOCABULARY

better	aHla, aHsan
birthday	9iid mileed
climate	maneex
cold	Sa'9a (related to weather)
especially	xSuuSan
feast	9iid
fog	GTayTa
healthy	SuHHi
historical sites	asaraat
history	teriix
hot	ʃawb (related to weather)
humidity	rTuube

moon	'amar
mountain	jabal
new	jdiid
old	'adiim
planet	kawkab
sometimes	aw'eet
star	nijme
sun	ʃams
village	Day9a

Chapter XV: Courtesy Expressions & Interjections

HAPPY OCCASIONS (afraaH)

Engagement (xuTbe)

- mabruuk   congratulations
- xuTbe mbaarake   may your engagement be blessed

Wedding (zaweej, 9urs)

- mabruuk ya 9ariis   congratulations groom
- mabruuk ya 9aruus   congratulations bride
- nʃalla btithannu   wishing you happiness
- kil iyyeemkun afraaH   may all your days be happy
  9a'beelak, 9a'beelik....   may your turn come

Birth (wileede)

- mabruuk-TTufl   congratulations on the baby
- *alla y9ayyʃu   may God give him a long life
- nʃalla byislam   may God keep him safe

Baptism, Christening (9meede)

- 9meede mbaarke   may this baptism be blessed

- nʃalla bit9ammdu-l'ixwe   may you baptize the siblings

Return from pilgrimage to Mecca (Hajj)

- Hajj mabruur   may your pilgrimage be blessed
  wsa9y maʃkuur   and your ritual walk be praise-
                         worthy

Success in business, career, or exam (najeeH)

- mabruuk   congratulations
- tahaniina   our best wishes
- *alla ywaffi'   may God grant you success

Holidays (a9yeed)

- kil 9iid w'inta bxayr   may every holiday you be
                             in good health
- 9iid mbaarak   happy (blessed) holiday

SAD OCCASIONS (aHzeen)

Accidents, tragedies (Haweedis, kaweeris)

- lHamdilla 9assaleeme   thank God for your safety
- *alla ySabbirkun   may God give you patience
- *alla y'awwikun   may God give you strength
- mniiH-lmiʃ a9Zam   lucky it was not worse

Sickness (maraD)

- saleemtak   wishing you feel better
- *alla yiʃfiik   may God give you a speedy
                           recovery
- *alla y'addimlak-   may God improve your
  SSuHHa   health

Death (mawt)

- *alla yirHamu   may God have mercy on him
- l9awaD bisaleemtak   may you be compensated by your well-being
- inna lillaah   we belong to God
- ta9aazina   our condolences

OTHER SOCIAL OCCASIONS (munesabeet ijtimee9iyye)

Going on a trip (safar)

- *alla ykuun ma9ak   may God be with you
- nʃalla tuSal bissaleeme   may you arrive safely
- safra mwaff'a   have a successful trip
- truuH wtirja9 bissaleeme   may you go and return safely

Return from a trip (rjuu9 min-ssafar)

- lHamdilla 9awSuulak bissaleeme
  thank God for your safe arrival

Moving to a new home (na'liyye)

- na'liyye mbaarke   hope this move was a blessed one
- mabruuk-lbayt   congratulations on the house

Coming out of the shower (duuʃ) or the barbershop (Hillee')

- na9iiman   hope you enjoyed it

At the table (9al'akl)

- Sahtayn   enjoy your food, bon appétit

- keesak   cheers, to your health
- sufra deeyme   may your table be always
                    bountiful (at the end of the meal)

If someone sneezes (9aTas)

- SuHHa   health
- naʃu   elation

If someone is wearing new clothes, or acquiring something new.

- mabruuk (lfustaan, ljizdeen, etc...)   congratulations

INTERJECTIONS

aH	reacting to something cold or hot
aax	expressing pain
bas	enough
nya9'	expressing disgust
oof	sigh of boredom or annoyance
tfeh	disgust or anger (similar to spitting)
Tuz	big deal, see if I care
yalla	come on, move it, hurry up
yaay	excitement, admiration
xay	sigh of relief, or smelling good aroma
9ayb	shame, disgrace

BODY LANGUAGE

Raising eyebrows, head or shoulders is a negative answer. This may be accompanied by the sound /tse/ , produced by the tongue rubbing roughly backward on the upper teeth and the palate.

Nodding head and raising eyebrows is a sign of admiration. This may be accompanied by the sound /biʃ/.

INDEX

The following is a list of all the verbs covered in the book. Verbs in bold character have been conjugated in the Grammar Notes Section of the corresponding chapter.

Chapter II: Socializing and Family Members

to be honored	tʃarraf
to come in	**tfaDDal**
to drink	**ʃirib**
to introduce	**9arraf**
to like, to love	**Habb**
to thank	**ʃakar**

Chapter III: Dates and Numbers

to arrive	**wuSil**
to be	**keen**
to enjoy	**nbasaT**
to enter	feet
to go	raaH
to have	ma9 or 9ind + pronominal suffixes
to return	riji9
to start	ballaʃ
to stay	**bi'i**

Chapter IV: Telephone and Post Office

to be lost	**Daa9**
to contact	**ttaSal**
to do	**9imil**
to give	**9aTa**
to hear	simi9

to leave	tarak
to phone, to call	**talfan**
to put	**HaTT**
to raise, to lift	**9alla**
to say	**'eel**
to send	**ba9at**
to speak	**Hiki**
to want	raad
to want	**badd**
to weigh	**wazan**

Chapter V: Biographical Information and Means of Transportation

to bet, to negotiate	ʃaaraT
to be able	**'idir**
to come	**ija**
to reside	sakan
to spend	**maDDa**
to take	**axad**
to use	**sta9mal**
to work	ʃtaGal

Chapter VI: Directions and Road Conditions

to ask	**sa'al**
to continue	kaffa
to cross	**'aTa9**
to exit, to go up	**Tuli9**
to go down	nizil
to guide, to show	dall
to find, to meet	**lee'a**
to know	**9irif**
to lose	**Dayya9**
to pay attention	**ntabah**
to see	ʃeef

to slow down	**xaffaf**
to stop	wa"af

Chapter VII: Food and Nutrition

to bring	**jeeb**
to chop, to mince	**faram**
to eat	akal
to invite	9azam
to order	**amar**
to prefer	faDDal
to prepare	HaDDar

Chapter VIII: Clothing

to become	Saar
to be confused	Htaar
to be invited	n9azam
to cut	'aSS
to fix, to repair	ZabbaT
to forget	**nisi**
to live	9eeʃ
to load up	Hammal
to match	libi'
to meet with	**tlee'a**
to prefer	faDDal
to travel	**seefar**
to wear	**libis**

Chapter IX: Health and Medical Problems

to appear	bayyan
to be hurting	**wiji9**
to believe	Sadda', 9ta'ad
to cough	sa9al
to describe	waSaf

to die	meet
to feel	Hass
to hurt, to injure	rawwaH
to limp	9araj
to prescribe	**waSaf**
to sleep	**neem**
to stay too long	Tawwal
to stitch, to sew	'aTTab
to wound	jaraH
to x-ray, to draw	Sawwar

Chapter X: Professions and Careers

to be a candidate	'addam 9ala...
to convey	waSSal
to finish	xallaS
to graduate	txarraj
to leave	tarak
to present	'addam
to protect	Himi
to remain, to stay	**Dall**
to specialize	txaSSaS
to study	daras

Chapter XI: Housing and Living Conditions

to agree with	**ttafa'**
to blame, to mind	weexaz
to bless	beerak
to congratulate	**beerak**
to enjoy	**thanna**
to furnish	faraʃ
to pass by	**mara'**
to pay	dafa9
to show	**farja**
to sit, to stay	**'a9ad**

| to stop | wa''af |

Chapter XII: Hobbies and Leisure Activities

to applaud	za''af
to attend, to watch	HuDir
to be able	'idir
to be late	**t'axxar**
to change	Gayyar
to dine	**t9aʃʃa**
to let	xalla
to play an instrument	da''
to reserve	Hajaz
to return something	radd
to sing	Ganna
to think	fakkar
to watch	tfarraj

Chapter XIII: Mishaps and Offenses

to appear	Zahar
to be caught	**9ili'**
to become distant	bi9id
to belong	xaSS
to extinguish	Taffa
to fear, to be afraid	**xaaf**
to inspect	kaʃaf
to jump	naTT
to put	HaTT
to request	Talab
to risk	xaaTar
to save someone	xallaS
to try	jarrab

Some incomplete verbs

Chapter XIV: Nature and Climate

to be bored	Dujir
to believe someone	Sadda'
to decide	**'arrar**
to get cold	Sa"a9
to play	li9ib
to smell	ʃamm
to swim	tsabbaH
to undergo changes	tGayyar
to visit	**zaar**